A TWEEN GIRL'S GUIDE TO FEELINGS & EMOTIONS

Mastering Self-Love
and Building Self-Esteem

The Essential Emotional Wellness Handbook
for Young Girls

Abby Swift

BEMBERTON
BOOKS

SOMETHING
FOR YOU

Thanks for buying this book. To show our appreciation, here's a **FREE** printable copy of the "Life Skills for Tweens Workbook"

WITH **OVER** 80 FUN ACTIVITIES **JUST FOR TWEENS!**

 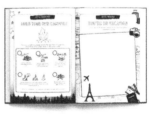

Scan the code to download your FREE printable copy

TABLE OF CONTENTS

INTRODUCTION

"When dealing with people, remember you are not dealing with creatures of logic, but with creatures of emotion."
— Dale Carnegie

Being a tween is anything but simple. With all the emotional roller-coasters, physical changes, and growth happening during puberty, it's a time full of challenges. One of the most crucial skills you can develop during this time is mastering your emotions. However, despite its importance, emotional development often doesn't get enough attention.

That's where "A Tween Girl's Guide to Feelings & Emotions" comes in. This book aims to help you understand your emotions better and boost your emotional intelligence. These skills are key to making your teen years smoother, helping you tackle the tough emotions and situations you might face.

Tweens and teens have a lot on their plates, from school and family to social lives and activities. With so much going on, learning about emotions might not seem like a priority. However, experts in education and psychology stress that social-emotional skills are incredibly important — sometimes even more so than academic skills. Emotionally intelligent kids tend to do better in school, have better relationships, and are more empathetic.[1]

If you haven't focused much on developing these skills yet, don't worry — it's never too late to start. "A Tween Girl's Guide to Feelings & Emotions" is designed to be your roadmap through this complex world of feelings. It's packed with discussions, exercises, and activities that not only help you understand your emotions, but also provide you with the tools you need to grow emotionally.

One key component of emotional development is opening yourself up to discussion. Discussions with family, peers, and people you trust, as well as having honest conversations with yourself, are essential for emotional growth. A big part of emotional development also involves learning how to navigate difficult conversations and uncomfortable situations in a healthy way.

"A Tween Girl's Guide to Feelings & Emotions" is an interactive book. Throughout the book, you'll find exercises, activities, and reflections to use and

---

1   *Teaching Emotional Intelligence in Early Childhood | NAEYC*

interact with. When you see the worksheet symbol, it's time to do the corresponding worksheets. Simply scan the QR code below to access these worksheets. Try to complete these activities, as they will help you develop a deeper understanding of yourself and your emotions, as well as teach you the tools needed to process your emotions and interact with others.

Top Tip

Take your time with this book and enjoy the process of learning more about yourself and your emotional intelligence. The skills you learn from this guide will serve you your entire life and can be applied repeatedly in numerous situations. It can feel uncomfortable to sit with your emotions and frightening to reflect on strong feelings, but only by doing so can you really develop a relationship with your emotions and learn how to process and control them healthily.

Scan this QR code to receive the free accompanying worksheets, which correspond to the activities in the book.

UNLOCKING EMOTIONAL INTELLIGENCE

Have you ever wondered why one day something makes you extremely mad or frustrated, but another day the same thing doesn't seem to bother you? Your reactions to events and situations aren't random; they're controlled by your emotional intelligence, or EI for short. Think of your EI as a compass guiding you through your day. Like a captain sailing a boat, you are the leader of your life.

Like a compass, your emotions provide positive and negative signals telling you how to feel and which way to go. However, if you misread your emotional compass, you may steer yourself into a storm!

As captain, it is essential to understand your emotions and develop a strong EI so you can read your compass successfully and navigate each day. If your compass is broken and you don't know how to read it, you'll struggle to keep your boat on course!

DID YOU KNOW?

Your emotional intelligence directly relates to your ability to handle stress, manage life changes, and develop and maintain healthy relationships with others.

What Is Emotional Intelligence?

You possess many types of intelligence. You may be good at math, excel at sports, be musically talented, or have strong writing skills. These are all examples of different types of intelligence. Emotional intelligence is your ability to interact with others, handle your emotions, and respond to them. It means being able to respond appropriately to others in different situations.

For example, imagine you're working on a group project at school and there's a disagreement. Strong EI allows you to recognize your frustration without letting it take over, communicate your thoughts calmly, and listen to your classmates' ideas.

Now, imagine a different scenario. You find out about a party that everyone seems to be invited to — except you. EI helps you manage disappointment, embarrassment, sadness, and anger.

Developing emotional intelligence also means learning how to respond correctly to challenging situations. For instance, if you fail a test after studying hard, emotional intelligence helps you understand that yelling at the teacher isn't the right approach, even if you believe the test was unfairly difficult. Instead, it guides you to process your feelings and then calmly discuss the test with your teacher.

EI plays a crucial role in many aspects of life, including school, friendships, family, and social interactions. Without well-developed EI, you might struggle to react appropriately in social and emotional situations. While some people may naturally have a high level of emotional intelligence, others need to work to develop it. However, everyone can improve their EI by learning and practicing specific skills. Remember, like any skill, some days it will be easier to apply your EI than others, as it can be affected by your overall well-being and environment.

Your emotional intelligence works like a gas tank — some days, it is full, and others, it needs fuel and maintenance.

Have you ever felt "hangry?" Hangry means angry because you're hungry. It is a perfect example of your tank needing fuel! If you're hungry, your blood sugar is low, making you cranky, irritable, and more likely to handle situations poorly.

The opposite happens when your tank is full. If you've slept well, scored an A on a test, or made the soccer team, your emotional tank is full and you can handle stressful situations better. Self-care is another way to keep your emotional tank full. Hanging out with friends, enjoying your favorite hobbies, and spending time with loved ones are all great ways to keep your EI topped up.

Emotional Intelligence consists of five key components:

- **Empathy:** This allows you to understand why a friend is upset over something that didn't directly affect you.

- **Social Skills:** These are crucial for interacting appropriately with others, such as not shouting in class or cutting off your friends mid-conversation.

- **Self-Awareness:** This helps you recognize your own feelings and reactions, such as why you might bounce your knee when you are anxious or feel queasy before a big event.

- **Self-Regulation:** This is about managing intense emotions, ensuring you don't lash out physically or burst into tears under stress.

- **Motivation:** This fuels your ambition to achieve goals, such as making the sports team or landing the solo in the spring concert.

Understanding how all five components work together and building upon your strengths is how you develop strong emotional intelligence. Now that you know the basics of EI and its importance, let's dive into each of the five components, starting with empathy.

"When awareness is brought to an emotion,
power is brought to your life."
— Tara Meyer Robson

EMPATHY

Empathy is the ability to understand and share the feelings of others. Empathy is a critical human skill because it allows you to show compassion to others. By employing empathy, you can temporarily set your needs and wants aside and look at a situation from someone else's point of view. For example, imagine you and your best friend tried out for the school play. You are cast in the lead, and your friend receives a small part. You feel excited, but your friend may be sad or disappointed. Empathy allows you to set aside your emotions temporarily and see things from your friend's point of view.

SOCIAL SKILLS

Social skills are your ability to interact with other people. Social skills include [2]:

- · Listening skills
- · Conversation skills
- · Manners

- · Self-control
- · Cooperation
- · Assertion

A solid grasp of what's appropriate and when and how to interact with others is essential to developing EI. Your EI helps you function at school and in social situations. For example, you understand that being responsible means arriving to class on time or offering support to someone who's being teased.

---

2   *What Are Social Skills? (Definition, Examples & Importance) (socialself.com)*

Self-Awareness

Self-awareness is perceiving who you are as a person. It is about truly understanding yourself as an individual, including your personality, actions, values, beliefs, emotions, and thoughts.[3]

You have public and private self-awareness. Your public self-awareness controls how you behave in most social situations.

Public self-awareness is how you behave at:

- School
- Church
- Social situations
- Playing sports or performing

Private self-awareness is something only you experience. Examples of private self-awareness include:

- Looking in the mirror
- Feeling nervous before singing a solo
- Remembering you forgot to study for a test
- Feeling butterflies in your stomach when you see your crush

Take a moment to think about the different emotions you've felt this week and what caused them. Did you feel excitement because your favorite team won? Or perhaps you felt disappointed when your

---

3   *Self-Awareness: Development, Types, and How to Improve (verywellmind.com)*

parents said you couldn't attend a party this weekend? Reflecting on these emotions is self-awareness.

Self-Regulation

Self-regulation is the mind's ability to control thoughts, functions, mental states, and inner processes. It means controlling our feelings and thoughts even when we don't want to!

Toddlers have tantrums because they lack self-regulation skills. Teens and tweens like you have much better self-regulation skills than little kids. You know not to throw your dinner on the floor if you don't like it, and you won't cry over getting the blue cup instead of the green one.

Self-regulation is key to reacting appropriately, especially in tense situations. It helps us avoid responses that we might regret later.

Motivation

Motivation comprises three things:

- **Activation:** The decision to start taking action or initiate a behavior.
- **Persistence:** The continued effort to achieve a goal and overcome obstacles.

- **Intensity:** The concentration and focus that goes into pursuing a goal.

Motivation is *why* you choose to do something. There are two types of motivation: intrinsic and extrinsic.

- **Intrinsic motivation** is personal motivation from within yourself — for example, reading a book for enjoyment or going for a walk to relax.

- **Extrinsic motivation** comes from an outside source. You usually receive an award of money, praise, awards, or social recognition. Examples of extrinsic motivation are studying for a test to get a good grade or doing chores to earn your allowance.

The Importance of Emotional Intelligence

EI is an essential skill to learn. Like all skills, some people are better at it than others.

Do you know anyone on the autism spectrum or who has ADHD? People with autism or ADHD tend to have lower levels of EI or emotional quotient (EQ).[4] This means they don't always know how to respond in social situations. For example, they may say inappropriate things, fail to make eye contact, or interrupt and talk out of turn.

---

4   How does EQ impact neurodivergent professionals? (welcometothejungle.com)

However, having a lower EQ doesn't equate to lower intelligence. Many neurodivergent individuals with challenges in EI shine in other areas, like math, science, music, or art.

Famous Neurodivergent People [5, 6]

- Albert Einstein (scientist)

- Emma Watson (actor)

- Nikola Tesla (inventor/scientist)

- Bobby Fischer (chess master)

- Bill Gates (business owner/inventor)

- Andy Warhol (artist)

- Justin Timberlake (musician)

- Pablo Picasso (artist)

- Simone Biles (gymnast)

- Emily Dickinson (poet)

---

5   *Successful People with Neurodivergent Disabilities — Student News (manchester.ac.uk)*

6   *Neurodiversity: The Definitive Guide | Ongig Blog*

The great news is that even if you struggle with EI, there are ways you can improve it! Like developing any skill, improving your EI takes time. Much like learning to play a musical instrument, you won't perform a flawless solo right away. It takes time, effort, and hard work.

EI is uniquely human. As far as we know, animals do not possess it. It is one of the earliest skills humans begin developing, alongside language. It is such a crucial skill that preschool and kindergarten teachers say that a child learning social-emotional skills is more important than mastering the basics like the alphabet or counting.

Workplaces are also starting to recognize the importance of emotional competence. While you're still young, there's no better time to develop the EI skills that future employers are looking for in young hires.

TWEEN GIRLS AND EMOTIONAL DEVELOPMENT

During your tween years, both your body and mind undergo significant changes. You might find yourself riding a rollercoaster of emotions, feeling one way one moment and completely different the next. This whirlwind of feelings is perfectly normal, even though it can sometimes be frustrating. Remember, it's all part of growing up.

As a tween, your mind and body are still developing. This journey of change will continue over the next few years. In fact, science tells us that our brains continue to develop into our 20s![7] Even at 18, when you're considered an adult, your brain is still in its adolescent stage of growth.

For girls, physical changes tend to occur earlier than for boys (though the emotional changes you experience may be quite similar). It's natural to have lots of questions about these changes, and you might notice their impact on your self-esteem or confidence levels.

---

7   *At What Age Is The Brain Fully Developed? — MentalHealthDaily*

It's crucial to understand that all these shifts are normal, driven by the hormones active in your body during this time.

As you enter puberty, your body gets flooded with hormones, which triggers the many changes your body undergoes.

This is important to understand, because much of what you're experiencing is part of a gradual process influenced by factors beyond your control. Remember, mastering your emotions doesn't happen overnight. Many adults are still working on their emotional skills. The good news is that, as a tween or teen, you're already ahead of where you were as a younger child when it comes to managing your emotions.

To navigate your ever-changing emotions, consider practices like meditation, yoga, deep breathing exercises, and journaling. Physical activities such as walking or dancing, spending quality time with friends, and engaging in your favorite hobbies or activities can also be incredibly beneficial.

Sometimes, just recognizing that your emotions are influenced by your body's changes and hormonal shifts can help you pause, reflect, and regain your calm.

Teen Emotional Skills

- Empathy: Understanding the feelings of others.

- Recognizing and naming different emotions: Identifying your and others' feelings and emotions.

- Impulse control: Being able to pause, think, and control your reactions.

- Maintaining friendships: Building strong friendship bonds.

- Understanding right from wrong: Developing a clear understanding of what is and is not acceptable.

- Patience: Developing the ability to wait, including coping with the frustration of delays.

- Problem-solving: Resolving issues thoughtfully.

As your hormones fluctuate and change, you may also begin experiencing some less pleasant emotions and changes[8]:

- Mood swings

- Concern about your appearance or clothes

- Short temper with siblings and parents

- Lack of confidence in physical appearance or abilities

---

8   *Young Teens (12–14 years old) | CDC*

- Sadness or even depression

- Peer pressure

- Confusion and uncertainty

Emotional Intelligence Basics [9]

- Everyone has feelings: We all have emotions and a built-in level of EI.

- Improves relationships: Developing your EI improves your relationships with others.

- Builds confidence: Strong social-emotional skills give you self-confidence.

- Social skills can be learned.

- Social rules vary: What's acceptable changes based on the situation.

- Being shy is fine: It's okay to be shy, but you can't avoid all social situations.

- Builds communication skills: Strong social-emotional skills equal strong communication skills.

- Helps you in everything: Your social-emotional health affects your school performance, mood, and physical health.

---

9   *What Are Social Skills? (Definition, Examples & Importance) (socialself.com)*

Discovering Your Strengths

Before you start working on understanding and managing your emotions, it's really important to figure out what you're good at. Think about the things you enjoy and excel in. Are you a fantastic singer, or can you play the piano beautifully? Maybe you're a whiz in subjects like science or history, or perhaps you have a talent for painting or helping others with patience and kindness. Recognizing these strengths does more than just make you feel good about yourself — it lays a solid foundation. When you know what you're good at and feel confident about it, you're in a much better position to tackle the challenge of improving how you handle your feelings and emotions.

 ## Discovering Your Strengths Worksheet

Take a moment to write down your strengths. These could be skills like playing soccer or writing, or traits that make up your personality, such as being funny, helpful, or compassionate. List them all out, whatever they may be.

Next, make a separate list of everything you like about yourself. Focus on your abilities, strengths, and achievements, rather than how you look. Some items might overlap with your strengths, and some might be different — and that's perfectly fine.

Once you have both lists, take a good look at them and identify anything that might relate to your EI. Traits like patience, kindness, politeness, problem-solving skills, effective communication, making friends easily, and the ability to learn new skills all contribute to EI.

Now that you have a better idea of your strengths, you can use them to enhance your emotional intelligence. Likewise, you'll better understand your weaknesses, and can start turning them into strengths, boosting your EI.

Fostering Personal Growth

To grow and learn, we often have to step outside our comfort zone and do something uncomfortable or even a little scary. Our comfort zone is like a safety net — it's the place we feel most secure. Perhaps you're used to playing goalkeeper, and your soccer coach moves you to play midfield for one game. Suddenly, you're in a new, unfamiliar position, unsure of what's expected of you.

Or maybe you're scared of snakes, but you visit the zoo and attend a demonstration where you can pet a snake. Do you step outside your comfort zone or hide at the back of the room? Often, it's much easier to try things that make us uncomfortable in a safe and secure environment.

Trying new things or stepping outside your comfort zone might feel uncomfortable. It is often hardest when you're worried you'll fail, be embarrassed, or get hurt.

You might fear embarrassing yourself, not being good at something, or failing. There are so many worries!

You'll only know if you try. Success, learning, and growth come from taking that leap. Think of something you're good at, like a sport, drawing, or cooking. Now, try to remember what it was like the first, second, or even fifth time you tried it. You probably weren't an instant expert! The reason you weren't good is that it was a new skill. But with practice and hard work, what was new and challenging became easier, more enjoyable, and something you're now good at.

Learning EI is the same. Only now, with the strengths you've already identified, you have a foundation to build upon to expand your EI.

DEVELOPING EMOTIONAL INTELLIGENCE

Using your strengths, you can begin to enhance your EI.

Controlling Emotions

One of the first steps is learning to name and control your emotions. You can do this by expressing your feelings. If you enjoy writing, use a journal to track your emotions. If you'd rather talk, chat with someone you trust about your feelings. And if you're an artist, you can paint, draw, or dance out your emotions! The more you express your feelings, the better you'll understand them and be able to control them.

Developing Empathy

Another crucial step is looking at situations from other people's point of view. This is called empathy, and it allows you to step back from a situation and see it differently. [10]

---

10   Emotional Intelligence (for Teens) — Nemours KidsHealth

For example, if you're mad at your little brother for barging into your room without knocking, think about why he came in. Does he want to play with you? Is he excited to show you something? This is the perfect opportunity to practice controlling your emotions and using empathy.

Building Your Social Skills

Building your social skills means working on your interactions with others. A great way to enhance your social skills is to interact with other people more. Find people you can compliment or help — even strangers!

10 Tips for Great Conversations

1 LISTEN ATTENTIVELY
Pay attention without interrupting.

6 STAY POSITIVE
Focus on uplifting topics.

2 ASK OPEN-ENDED QUESTIONS
Encourage meaningful discussions.

7 PRACTICE ACTIVE LISTENING
Engage and show you value their input.

3 SHARE EXPERIENCES
Connect by sharing stories.

8 STAY CURIOUS
Ask questions and learn from others.

4 BE EMPATHETIC
Show understanding and support.

9 MIND YOUR BODY LANGUAGE
Maintain good posture and eye contact.

5 RESPECT DIFFERENCES
Be open-minded and respectful.

10 END POSITIVELY
End with thanks & leave the door open for future talks.

Engaging in conversations is another way to build your social skills. Find people with shared interests to talk to, or start a conversation with someone while waiting in line at the store (or with your favorite teacher before class begins).

Practice Active Listening

Active listening helps you develop empathy and conversation skills. Show you are listening by repeating details back to the person who is speaking. Maintain eye contact and face the person while they speak to you. Do your best not to interrupt or turn the conversation about yourself.

Ways to Build Emotional Intelligence

- Think about things from different points of view.

- Talk to people more.

- Try new things.

- Express your emotions.

- Engage in mindfulness (yoga, exercise, meditation).

- Focus on and use your strengths.

- Practice being assertive (when appropriate), saying "No" to things you don't want to do.

- Learn your body's non-verbal cues (for example, do you roll your eyes, cross your arms, or sigh when frustrated?).

- Accept your emotions (there are no bad emotions!).

REMEMBER!

Your EI is under construction. It grows, changes, and improves as you develop and age. The more you practice your social-emotional skills, the quicker and easier they'll develop.

EXPLORING YOUR EMOTIONS

*"Our emotions need to be as educated as our intellect.
It is important to know how to feel, how to respond,
and how to let life in so that it can touch you."*
— Jim Rohn, *Motivational Speaker*

Emotions are a natural state of being. As a human, you are constantly feeling and experiencing emotions. You might be bored in class or excited about your upcoming game. You may be nervous about a first date or happy it is Friday afternoon.

Human philosophers, psychologists, and scientists have been trying to define and explain human emotions since the time of the ancient Greek philosopher Aristotle (4th century B.C.E.). According to Aristotle, humans experience 14 different base emotions[11]:

⭐ FEAR	⭐ INDIGNATION	⭐ PITY
⭐ ENMITY	⭐ ANGER	⭐ CONTEMPT
⭐ ENVY	⭐ SHAMELESSNESS	⭐ CALM
⭐ CONFIDENCE	⭐ EMULATION	⭐ KINDNESS
⭐ SHAME	⭐ FRIENDSHIP	

In 1872, naturalist and biologist Charles Darwin theorized that humans only experienced five emotions[12]: fear, anger, sadness,

---

11   *How Many Human Emotions Are There? (verywellmind.com)*

12   *Basic Emotions: A Reconstruction — William A. Mason, John P. Capitanio, 2012 (sagepub.com)*

happiness, and love. However, 130 years later, Robert Plutchick believed humans experienced more than 90 different emotions![13]

The currently accepted theory, put forth by psychologist Paul Eckman, narrows the list to seven base emotions[14], including happiness, sadness, fear, and anger. Eckman's theory suggests that these seven emotions are the foundation from which all other emotion variations derive.

The table below lists the six most common basic human emotions. Fill in the chart with as many versions of the same emotion as possible.

Happiness	Sadness	Fear	Anger	Disgust	Surprise
Confidence Love		Anxiety	Frustration Hurt		

---

13   The Nature of Emotions: Human emotions have deep evolutionary roots, a fact that may explain their complexity and provide tools for clinical practice on JSTOR

14   How Many Emotions Can You Feel? | Psychology Today

If you're a fan of Disney-Pixar movies, you might recognize these basic emotions from "Inside Out." The film explores tween Riley's mind as she navigates the challenges of moving to a new city and making new friends. She experiences anger toward her parents for the move, sadness for missing her friends and ice hockey, and fear of attending a new school and living in an unfamiliar place, among other feelings. The film provides a glimpse into the emotional rollercoaster a tween can experience.

It's entirely possible to feel all of these emotions in one day. You may even feel them in a matter of hours or even minutes, depending on the situation you're experiencing.

Tweens and teens often have trouble identifying and connecting emotions to their thoughts and experiences. However, as Jim Rohn's quote earlier in the chapter points out, understanding your emotions is key. He says, "It is important to know how to feel, how to respond, and how to let life in so that it can touch you." Mastering your feelings allows you to fully experience all that life has to offer!

Identifying Emotions

It's usually clear when you're experiencing happiness, sadness, or anger, and the sensations of surprise or disgust are familiar, too. Chances are, you can recall many instances when you've felt each of the seven fundamental emotions: happiness, sadness, fear, anger, disgust, surprise, and love.

But you have probably also experienced situations where you weren't exactly sure what you felt, and the emotion was incorrectly labeled as something else. Labeling our emotions can be tricky, especially in highly charged emotional moments.

Are you familiar with the Harry Potter series by J. K. Rowling? The fifth book, "Harry Potter and the Order of the Phoenix", is often referred to as being full of teenage angst and emotion. The main characters are now 14 and 15 years old. On top of trying to stop an evil wizard from returning to power, they're dealing with puberty, social situations, school, and family pressures. When you read the books, you can see the whirlwind of emotions. Each feeling piles on top of another, making it impossible to separate, understand, and identify them individually.

Humans are capable of feeling a range of emotions, but emotions are like colors that blend into each other. Sometimes, fear might also feel like worry. Likewise, happiness might feel like peace or confidence. When basic emotions don't fully explain how we're feeling, an emotion wheel can help.

Using an Emotion Wheel

An emotion wheel is like a map that shows many different feelings. It helps us find the exact word that matches our emotions. If you're feeling something but can't quite describe it, the emotion wheel can help you better understand yourself. It's a handy tool for exploring all the feelings that bubble up inside us, making it easier to see and name each one.

Trying to figure out and understand your emotions, just like in the Harry Potter books, is often challenging! So, how do you identify confusing and unfamiliar emotions? With patience, practice, and getting to know yourself better!

Getting to Know Yourself

To better understand your emotions, you must get to know yourself better. How does your brain work? What situations do you handle easily, and which do you find stressful?

Take a few minutes to take the Emotion Quiz to discover which base emotion you connect with the most.

 **Getting to Know Yourself Worksheet**

After taking the quiz, were you surprised by the results, or did it sound just like you? Remember, these quizzes are mostly for insight, and are not an official diagnosis or indicator of any medical or mental health condition. Nonetheless, answering the questions honestly gives you a good idea of how you respond emotionally to situations.

Connecting Emotions and Thoughts

Part of getting to know yourself is connecting your thoughts with the emotions you are experiencing. Our thoughts and emotions are internal, but they influence our external actions and behaviors. For example, you might feel angry because your sister borrowed your favorite sweatshirt without asking, so you go into her room and yell at her. Or, you might be frustrated while studying for your science test, so you slam the book shut and throw it on the floor.

When you understand your emotions, you can better control your actions and make them situationally appropriate. This means you'll be able to behave appropriately for the place you're at and the people you're with.

There is nothing wrong with crying, being angry, showing nerves, etc., but you may not wish to cry in front of your peers for failing a test, and you know that punching a wall is inappropriate.

A lot of times, strong emotions cause us to respond without thinking. If you're able to understand your emotions and their connection to specific behaviors, you'll learn how to slow your brain down and think before responding.[15]

Ready for another quiz? Try the worksheet to discover your emotional type.

 **Emotional Type Worksheet**

Knowing your emotional type gives you insight into how you respond to various situations. Once you understand your emotional type, you'll see how you mentally and physically react to emotional situations. The way your body physically responds is called body language. Our bodies can tell us and others a lot about what we are thinking and feeling!

---

15   *Relationship between thoughts, emotions and behaviours — Complete guide — Visit MHP*

Body Language and Sensations

Our bodies and faces can tell an entire story without us saying a single word! You probably engage in various actions or faces when experiencing emotions without realizing it.

Using the chart below, think of a time you felt each base emotion, then write down sensations in your body, actions you took, or any other thoughts related to the situation.

For example, when you are nervous, maybe you bounce your knee. Or, when you're excited, maybe you talk loudly and quickly.

When I Feel..	I...
Happy	
Sad	
Angry	
Scared	
Disgusted	
Surprised	
Love	

Journaling is another excellent way to connect your thoughts to your emotions. At the end of the day, spend five minutes journaling about an emotional experience you had that day.

You can write about a good or bad experience. Sometimes, we think big emotions are only negative, but they can also be joyous and exciting. For example, getting the lead in the school musical, scoring the winning goal, or being asked out by your crush are all reasons you might feel big emotions!

The Science of Emotions

Scientists have narrowed down the emotional range to what they call the Four Irreducible Emotions: happiness, sadness, anger, and fear.[16] These are the emotions we feel in our most basic, animal-like form.

Research says these are the four emotions we are all born with, and your cultural and social experiences influence the range of these four emotions you feel.

---

16   *How Many Human Emotions Are There? (verywellmind.com)*

DID YOU KNOW? A 2020 research study showed that humans have 16 universal facial expressions: [17]

- Amusement
- Anger
- Awe
- Concentration
- Confusion
- Contempt
- Contentment
- Desire

- Disappointment
- Doubt
- Elation
- Interest
- Pain
- Sadness
- Surprise
- Triumph

Pause and think about how you are sitting right now. Are your shoulders scrunched up or your teeth clenched? Have you rolled your eyes reading any of this? Perhaps you're fidgeting with a toy. These are all body language expressions you might not even know you're doing!

---

17 *Reading Facial Expressions: 7 Expressions, Interpret Them (verywellmind.com)*

CONTAGIOUS EMOTIONS

Science also tells us that emotions can spread from person to person. This is typically a subconscious action, meaning that you are unaware it is happening. [18]

Imagine being at a big game when your team scores. The wave of excitement that sweeps through everyone cheering is emotional contagion. Or, perhaps your teacher announces a test on Friday. Your best friend tells you they're nervous about this test after class. Suddenly, you find yourself feeling anxious, too!

Research indicates that people tend to feel happier when their friends are happy. [19] So, if you're feeling down, talking to a cheerful friend might help improve your mood. But remember, your emotions can also spread to others, so aim to share positive feelings!

Emotional Output Self-Reflection

- What emotions do I give off, and how does that affect others?

- Do I let others affect my emotions? Do I even know it is happening?

---

18 Emotions are contagious: Learn what science and research has to say about it — MSU Extension

19 SOCIAL NETWORKS AND HAPPINESS | Edge.org

- Are my friends positively or negatively affecting my emotions? Are these the people I really want to surround myself with?

- What changes could I make about how I express my emotions?

Are you interested to know how easily emotional contagion affects you? Take the quiz![20]

 **Emotional Contagion Worksheet**

Emotional Reflections

"You can't manage what you can't measure."

Regular emotional reflection is the best way to learn more about what you feel, how you feel it, and when you feel it. There are numerous ways to pause and reflect on your emotions. What works best for you will depend on your likes, interests, and dislikes.

- Journaling: Journaling is a private way to record your emotions and thoughts. It is also a very healthy way to express strong feelings.

---

20 *The Emotional Contagion Scale | Psychology Today*

- Emotional Tracking: Emotion or mood tracking helps you learn your triggers, control your emotions, and develop strategies to overcome strong emotions and negative or impulsive behaviors.

 **Emotional Tracker**

- Meditation/Mindfulness: Regular meditation and mindfulness activities help you connect with your feelings and inner thoughts. They are also a great way to calm down and re-center yourself when experiencing strong negative emotions. Check out YouTube for meditations made especially for kids and teens!

- Listening to or Playing Music: Music is an emotional experience. Find music that mirrors your mood or the mood you want to feel. If you play an instrument, sing, or dance, do one of those activities to connect with your emotions and feelings.

REMEMBER! You must understand and identify your emotions to control and react to them appropriately. Take time to get to know yourself better. Learn your natural emotional responses and reflect on your nonverbal expressions, such as body language and facial expressions. Reflecting on your emotions each day is the best way to learn about them.

EXPRESSING YOUR FEELINGS

"Control what you can control. I can control my emotions, my attitude, and my effort every day."
— Michael Trubisky, Athlete

The quote above is from Michael Trubisky, an NFL quarterback who played for the Chicago Bears and Pittsburgh Steelers. Sports are often highly emotional for those playing and watching. Tempers often flare, and so does excitement. Playing sports at a high level teaches players to control strong emotions and express them healthily.

Yelling at a referee or screaming in a coach's face are inappropriate ways for athletes to show frustration and may result in them getting benched and taking an early shower. Instead, they can choose to accept the decision, even if they don't like it, vent to a teammate, and then use that disappointment to get back out there and try again. These are all healthy ways to express emotion.

An angry athlete is an example of expressing feelings positively and negatively. Now, it's your turn! Think of a time recently when you felt a strong emotion.

Maybe you argued with one of your parents about not being allowed to go to a party, or you lost a battle in Fortnite with only you and one other player remaining. These are emotionally charged situations that often result in big expressions of emotion. Big, however, doesn't necessarily mean bad. Big emotions are OK as long as they are appropriate to the situation.

You can express big emotions positively or negatively, but the emotion itself isn't good or bad. There are no bad emotions, because all feelings are valid, even when they feel uncomfortable.

Think again about the recent situation where you felt strong emotions. How did you handle your emotions? Did you behave appropriately, or is there something you could have changed about your emotional expression? Did you slam a door when you could have taken a deep breath instead? Did you say something unkind instead of asking for space with your thoughts?

In this chapter, we will explore what emotional expression is and looks like, explore tips for controlling your emotions, and discuss healthy ways to express big emotions.

What Is Emotional Expression?

Emotional expression is how we verbally and non-verbally communicate our feelings to others. Most of us know when we feel angry, sad, or happy. But do you know what your body and face look like when you feel those emotions? Are you aware of any habits or things you commonly do when you feel specific emotions?

In the previous chapter, you practiced connecting your emotions to body sensations and body language. You also learned about yourself and how different emotions feel in your body.

Those feelings, sensations, and actions are all part of your emotional expressions. Most of the time, you are probably in control of your emotional expressions — but no one is *always* in control. Even adults lose their tempers, cry, and shout in excitement.

Some people like being alone when angry, while others yell or throw things. When you're nervous, maybe you bite your fingernails or snap at anyone who talks to you.

While some emotional expressions, like frowning or smiling, are common, everyone experiences and expresses emotions differently. What you see is not always the truth behind what someone is feeling.

We usually think of crying as a sad emotion, but many people also cry when happy. Some people may frown or scowl when thinking or are confused, while others smile, laugh, or joke when nervous.

Learning the many layers of emotional expression will help you better express yourself and represent your true feelings.

I felt angry because... (Describe the situation)	I felt sad because...	I felt overwhelmed because...
How I expressed it: (Eg. Did you shout, argue etc?)	How I expressed it:	How I expressed it:
Instead, I could have... (Explain how you could have reacted)	Instead, I could have...	Instead, I could have...

Use the chart above to think of three different times you felt a big emotion and didn't handle it as well as you could have. Describe what you did, your emotional expression, and a possible alternative solution. We listed angry, sad, and overwhelmed, but if you have an example of another big emotion, use that instead!

The exercise you just did allowed you to examine your current emotional expression tactics and techniques. Most of the time, you probably handle your emotions in healthy ways. For example, you don't yell at your mom when she asks you to clean your room or kick your little sister when she annoys you.

But, as a tween or teen, your emotions and ability to understand and express them are still developing. Just like developing any other skill, the more you practice, the better you'll become! Let's examine some healthy ways to express emotions and tips to keep yourself in control, even during the most emotional experiences!

Healthy Ways to Express Emotions

Expressing your emotions is super important. If you keep them all bottled up, they'll stagnate inside you. No matter how hard you try to keep them hidden, they'll burst out eventually — and often not in good ways. Keeping all those feelings inside can make you more stressed, bring down your mood, and even hurt your physical and mental health.

Imagine you're like a volcano that's ready to erupt. All that pressure just keeps building and building until it explodes. This explosion usually comes out as anger, even if you're feeling scared, embarrassed, sad, or jealous. When you let it all out like that, how you show your feelings doesn't match up with what you're truly feeling inside — and that's not a healthy way to deal with emotions. You might end up saying things you didn't mean, unfairly taking out your frustration on someone else, or acting in ways you regret later.

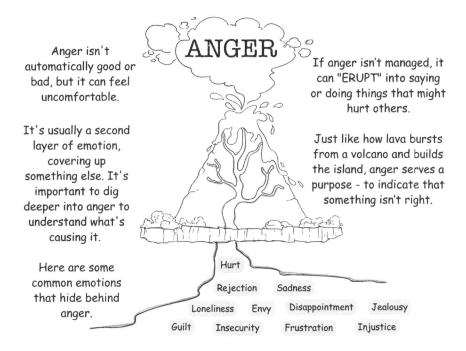

Anger isn't automatically good or bad, but it can feel uncomfortable.

It's usually a second layer of emotion, covering up something else. It's important to dig deeper into anger to understand what's causing it.

Here are some common emotions that hide behind anger.

ANGER

If anger isn't managed, it can "ERUPT" into saying or doing things that might hurt others.

Just like how lava bursts from a volcano and builds the island, anger serves a purpose - to indicate that something isn't right.

Hurt

Rejection   Sadness

Loneliness   Envy   Disappointment   Jealousy

Guilt   Insecurity   Frustration   Injustice

When emotions get bottled up, it's often the tough ones like anger that build up pressure. But it's key to remember that there's nothing wrong with feeling anger or any other emotion. Emotions aren't good or bad — they're just part of being human. Anger, for example, is a normal and healthy emotion. The real issue is how you choose to express that anger. If you don't figure out a positive way to show how you're feeling, you might express your emotions in an unhealthy manner.

Why We Experience Emotions Differently

Why do we all feel things so differently? It's because we're all unique — not just in how we see the world, but also in how we respond to it. A big part of how you handle your emotions comes from what you've seen growing up. If a parent or someone close to you gets angry and shouts or slams doors, you might do the same. But if you've seen someone stay cool and collected in tough times, you're more likely to pick up those calm vibes.

Your own body plays a role, too. For instance, people with ADHD might find themselves getting super mad really fast. Meanwhile, someone dealing with depression might not show much emotion at all. And if you're someone who gets anxious, stress can feel extra heavy. [21]

Here's the good news: Learning to express your feelings in a healthy way is a skill — and, like any skill, you can get better at it. But it'll take some effort and patience. You don't have to try every method

---

21   *The Biology of Emotions | Brain & Behavior Research Foundation (bbrfoundation.org)*

out there — just pick a few that seem like they might work for you and give them a shot. After a while, take a moment to reflect on times you felt really emotional and see if you handled things better. If not, no worries — just try something else. The key is to keep at it and not give up.

Activities to Improve Your Emotional Expression

- **Practice Gratitude:** People who are grateful experience less stress and more happiness. Gratitude reduces uncomfortable emotions like stress and anger and improves mental health.[22] Using a gratitude journal to write down a few things you're grateful for each day is an excellent way to express healthy emotions. If you're struggling with gratitude, try adding the phrase "I get to do this" to activities. For example, if you don't want to clean your room, say, "I have a safe home and a room of my own, and I get to do this!" This is called re-framing. Re-framing a situation helps you find the positive in a situation, and will remind you how lucky you are that you have a bedroom to make messy and have to clean!

- **Enjoy the Moment:** Try to really enjoy what you're doing in the moment. Many of us, especially teens and tweens, get swept up in capturing everything on our phones, like snapping selfies or videos. How about putting your phone aside and just

---

22 *Reprogram Your Brain for Happiness (psu.edu)*

soaking up the moment, without worrying about sharing it or posting online? Spending too much time on social media can actually make you feel worse about yourself, mess with your sleep, and even cut down on how much you move around, all of which can affect your mood and emotional well-being. [23]

- **Get Active:** Being physically active helps lower stress and increases your energy, leading to a better mood. When you're feeling good, it's much easier to express your emotions in a healthy way!

- **Spend Time Outdoors:** Spending time outdoors has been scientifically proven to improve your mental and physical health. [24] Whether gardening or engaging in other outdoor activities, being outside can lift your spirits and help you manage stress better. Even indoor gardening is excellent for your mental health and can teach you to be more empathetic by taking care of plants. [25]

- **Practice Mindfulness:** Mindfulness can help you calm your mind and deal with strong feelings by giving you a moment to pause between feeling and reacting. Taking time to quietly think about what you're feeling lets you understand and respond to your emotions in a healthy way. You can find mind-

23 *5 Ways Social Media Affects Kids' Mental Health (And How Parents Can Help!) — FamilyEducation*

24 *The wellness benefits of the great outdoors | US Forest Service (usda.gov)*

25 *Gardening is beneficial for health: A meta-analysis — ScienceDirect*

fulness exercises and meditations suited to different feelings on YouTube or meditation apps.

- **Get Creative**: Activities like listening to music, playing an instrument, dancing, drawing, and coloring can lower stress and help you process your emotions. Use your feelings as inspiration to create something unique, whether writing a story, painting a picture, or choreographing a dance. Turning your emotions into art is a positive way to express and understand them.

Techniques for Staying in Control During Emotional Expression

Everyone faces times when emotions run high and it's challenging to keep your cool. Maybe you've felt your temper flare up or been overwhelmed by frustration. Fortunately, there are strategies you can use to better manage your emotions during these intense moments:

- **Practice Empathy**: Empathy is the ability to look at a situation from another person's point of view. For example, imagine your best friend is upset because someone they like turned them down, and they come to you for comfort. Being empathetic means putting yourself in their shoes and feeling their disappointment.

- **Be an Active Listener**: The better you are at listening to others, the better your emotional expression will become. Don't rush the person talking so you can have a turn. Instead, listen to what they are saying and try to understand what they are telling or asking you.

- **Be Forgiving**: Choosing to forgive others is a sign of maturity and helps you let go of heavy emotions. Forgiveness doesn't mean you're okay with being hurt or wronged — it means you're choosing to move past those hard feelings in order to communicate and express yourself more effectively.

Practicing Healthy Expression

So far in this chapter, we've examined emotional expression, tips to improve your emotional expression abilities, and techniques for staying calm when experiencing big emotions. Now, we will examine some active steps you can take to practice healthy expression.

Just like you can't hit a home run in a game if you've never swung a bat before, you won't be able to express yourself effectively in emotional moments if you haven't practiced the skills.

- **Try an Emotional Checklist:** An emotional checklist asks you a series of questions to help you process big feelings. By answering the questions truthfully, you will gain an understanding of what's going on and find ways to express emotions in a healthy way.

 **Emotional Checklist**

- **Write or Draw About Your Emotions:** If you're experiencing powerful emotions, write about them or draw a picture. For example, imagine writing to the person who upset you, or draw a picture of your feelings. These activities provide clarity and help you practice expressing your feelings.

- **Talk to the Mirror:** Have practice conversations in the mirror. It may seem silly or weird, but talking it out to the mirror is an outlet to practice emotional expression. When you say something out loud, you might realize how hurtful it could sound, or that it doesn't adequately communicate your feelings. Pretend the person you need to talk to is right there in the mirror and say what you need to say!

- **Practice Empathy with Characters**: When you're reading a book or watching a movie and you hit an emotional scene, take a moment to pause. Think about what the characters are feeling. Write down your thoughts on each character's emotions, motivations, and whether their actions align with their intentions. Did they achieve what they wanted? Why or why not?[26]

· **Role Play with a Friend or Family Member**: If there's a tough conversation coming up that you know will stir up strong emotions, try practicing it with a friend, family member, or even a school counselor whom you trust. Whether it's talking about ending a relationship or expressing a change in interests, like not wanting to play the piano anymore after years of lessons, rehearsing what you'll say can be really beneficial.

The Power of Words

Words are powerful tools. While many animals communicate using sounds and signals, humans are the only species that has developed language. It is easy to take the gift of language for granted and forget its power.

You've probably heard the saying, "Sticks and stones may break my bones, but words will never hurt me." While it sounds reassuring, it's not always true. Words can be deeply hurtful, especially during intense emotional moments, and their effects can last a long time.

However, this doesn't mean you should keep your feelings to yourself. The key is choosing your words thoughtfully and with care. Expressing our emotions offensively or inappropriately can harm

---

26 Fostering-Empathy-Reflectively.pdf (b-cdn.net)

our relationships with others. For instance, if you feel overwhelmed about an audition and snap at your best friend to "shut up and go away," you will likely hurt their feelings.

Instead, if you say, "Hey, I'm really nervous and I need some space. Can we chat later?" a real friend will get where you're coming from and give you the space you need.

Choosing the right words — words that are safe and respect-ful — helps us feel closer to the people we care about. Knowing the best words to use and the right time to use them is crucial for keeping our relationships strong and healthy.

Steps to Choose Words and Expressions

1. **Take a Moment:** Before you say anything, pause and identify what you're feeling.

2. **Calm Down First:** Anger can make you defensive. If your feel-ings fall along the anger spectrum (mad, frustrated, annoyed, irritated, etc.), calm down before you start talking.

   ☞ Try a word other than "anger" for the feeling that re-mains, such as disappointed, sad, or scared. Using these types of words can decrease your defensiveness.

3. **Use "I Feel…" Statements:** Start sentences with "I feel…" to discuss your feelings without blaming anyone. For example, "I felt disappointed when you didn't show up as planned."

4. **Explain Why:** Provide more details about why you felt a certain way. "I felt disappointed because it made me feel like you didn't value my time or friendship."

Following these steps gives you space to think and choose words that clearly express how you feel, without causing blame or hurt. This approach can prevent arguments and helps ensure your message is understood.

Slowing things down can also help you manage difficult emotions by allowing you time to reflect and understand what you are feeling in the moment.

REMEMBER!

Sharing how you feel is good for you, and there's no such thing as a "bad" emotion. Some feelings are just bigger, stronger, or more uneasy than others. Learning how to stay calm, picking the right words, and getting better at showing your emotions will help you express yourself in a healthy way.

MANAGING DIFFICULT EMOTIONS

Sometimes, when we feel strong emotions, it's because we feel a situation is unfair, we're embarrassed, we're in pain (physically or emotionally), or we aren't feeling our best (like when we're tired, sick, or hungry). During these times, diving into our emotional toolbox and pulling out the necessary skills to keep our emotions in check is crucial.

In *Chapter 3: Expressing Your Feelings,* we explored ways to share how you're feeling and techniques for staying calm while doing so. This chapter will expand upon that theme and focus on managing difficult emotions.

Being open about your emotions is important, but it's just one piece of the puzzle. Knowing how to manage those emotions is equally important, especially when you can't talk about them right away — like during a nerve-wracking test or a high-stakes sports game.

Below, we'll introduce several strategies for effectively managing intense emotions when they arise. These techniques are tools for your emotional toolkit, ready to be used whenever you need them most!

Strategies for Difficult Emotions: Handling Stress, Anger, and Sadness

Dealing with emotions like stress, anger, and sadness is tough. It's something even adults find challenging. The first thing to keep in mind is that there are no "bad" emotions. Some emotions might make us feel uncomfortable, but that doesn't mean they're wrong to have.

Thinking of emotions as good or bad can make us feel like we're not supposed to experience certain ones. The truth is, all emotions are valid. The key is learning how to understand and navigate these feelings.

- **Accept What You Can't Change**: Learning to accept situations and other people is a big step in emotional maturity. For example, if you have to take a surprise quiz or don't make the sports team, focus on what you can control. This could mean staying on top of your schoolwork to be ready for quizzes or practicing more for the next tryouts.

- **Breathing Exercises:** When you feel stressed or overwhelmed, try controlled breathing to help your brain return to a calm place. Close your eyes, slowly breathe in through your nose for five counts, and then out through your mouth for five counts.

Place your hands on your belly to feel the breath entering and leaving your body.

- **Take a Break from the Situation:** Taking a break from the discussion, task, or activity provides time to pause and reflect. Saying something like, "Let's pause this discussion and come back to it later," gives everyone time to cool down. The more frustrated and emotional you become during an argument or activity, the less able you are to express yourself healthily.

- **Use an Emotional Checklist:** As we explored in *Chapter 3*, an emotional checklist can help you understand and identify your feelings. Sometimes, what seems like anger is disappointment or frustration. Understanding your true feelings is the first step in managing them effectively.

- **Use an Emotion Wheel:** If you're unsure what you might be feeling, use an emotion wheel to pinpoint your emotions.

Coping Techniques: Methods for Managing Fear, Anxiety, and Jealousy

Fear, anxiety, and jealousy can often disguise themselves as anger. This is because they're closely related emotions, and anger is a fundamental emotion we all know well. The ways to deal with sadness, anger, and stress can also help with anxiety, fear, and jealousy.

Breathing exercises, for example, are great tools for nearly any tough emotion. Deep breathing can calm your nerves and reduce fear and anxiety.

UNDERSTANDING JEALOUSY AND ENVY

Jealousy is a tricky emotion, and shouldn't be confused with envy.

JEALOUSY vs ENVY

Jealousy is when you're worried someone will take what's yours.

Envy is when you wish you had what someone else does.

-------EXAMPLES -------

- Feeling upset because your best friend is spending more time with someone else.
- Worrying your sibling is getting more attention from your parents.
- Being afraid your pet dog likes your brother/sister more.
- Concerned a classmate might get the lead role in the play that you wanted.

-------EXAMPLES -------

- Wanting the same smartphone your friend just got.
- Wishing you could score as well as your classmate on a math test.
- Wanting your neighbor's new bike.
- Hoping to get as many likes and followers on social media as your friend.
- Wanting the same cool backpack your teammate has.

- **Jealousy** is when you are afraid someone will take what you already have. For example, if you're worried about losing a solo in the spring concert to another student because you're sick, that's jealousy.

- **Envy** is when you want something that someone else has. When you see someone with the brand-new Nike sneakers you want and an uncomfortable feeling creeps in, that feeling is envy.

Tips to manage envy or jealousy:

- **It's Okay**: Remember that jealousy, in small doses, is a normal, healthy reaction.

- **Mindfulness:** Use mindfulness to work through your feelings.

- **Practice Gratitude:** Focus on what you have. Maybe you don't have the latest Nike shoes, but you got a lovely new dress last weekend.

- **Practice Positive Self-Talk**: Lift yourself up! Remind yourself of all your skills, talents, and great qualities.

- **Share Your Feelings**: Talk to someone about how you feel.

Dealing with Jealousy in Relationships

Feeling jealous, especially when it comes to relationships, might be something new for you as a tween or teen. You may be starting to find others attractive, or even beginning to date. It's important to know that jealousy can strain a relationship and affect how you feel about yourself.

Jealousy is a natural reaction that often comes from feeling threatened, like if someone is a bit too friendly with the person you're dating. Even if there's no real danger, it can still feel like a big deal to you.

If you've begun dating and are experiencing jealousy, here are some tips to help you manage your feelings before they grow out of control:

- It's okay to admit you are feeling jealous.

- Accept that, when left unchecked, jealousy can harm your relationship.

- Decide to work on your behavior and reactions.

- Trust your partner. Never spy on them.

- Discuss the roots of your jealous feelings.

- Understand that you cannot control someone else, but you can control how you respond to situations.

- Speak to a counselor, trusted adult, or therapist.

UNDERSTANDING AND PROCESSING GRIEF

Grief is a very uncomfortable and difficult emotion to manage, especially for young people. If you're fortunate, you might not have faced much grief yet — but if you have, you probably found it hard to understand and deal with those feelings.

We feel grief when we lose something. It could be because of the death of a pet, the end of a relationship, or moving away from a place you love. Grief changes over time and differs with each loss. You might feel overwhelming grief when a pet dies, but only a small amount of grief if you lose something like your favorite necklace.

Despite these differences, there are ways to manage grief, no matter the situation. Here's a look at how to navigate through the grieving process:

- **Talk to Someone:** Find someone to talk to. It can be a friend, parent, teacher, counselor, or religious leader.

- **Express Your Feelings:** Try journaling or expressing your grief through art or music.

- **Allow Yourself to Grieve:** Remember that grief is normal. It is OK to feel grief.

- **Don't Bottle It Up:** If you've lost a loved one, find ways to keep their memory alive. Listen to their favorite music, keep pictures of them around, and talk about them.

- **Take a Break from Social Media:** Avoid discussing your grief on social media platforms. Expressions of grief on social media can be twisted and altered by rumors or people who don't know what you're feeling, which may make the grieving process harder.

- **Write a Goodbye Letter:** Writing a letter to the person or thing you are grieving can be a powerful way to process your feelings.

 **Goodbye Letter Worksheet**

- **Use a Stages of Grief Worksheet to Help You Process Your Emotions:** The stages of grief can happen in any order, and you can bounce around between them many times, but acceptance always comes last.
  - Stages of Grief:
    - ☞ Denial: Not accepting that it has happened.
    - ☞ Anger: Being angry at the person, God, someone else, or even yourself that it has happened.
    - ☞ Bargaining: You want to create an alternate situation where it didn't happen.
    - ☞ Depression: Feeling sad and hopeless about it.
    - ☞ Acceptance: Learning to be OK that it happened.

Breathing Exercises and Mindfulness Techniques

We've discussed breathing exercises and mindfulness several times already in this book, and that's because they're handy tools for calming down and reflecting on one's emotions.

Here are some excellent breathing exercises and mindfulness techniques for managing tough emotions anywhere, anytime!

Breathing Exercises

- **8-4-7 Breathing**: The 8-4-7 exercise is very common and can be done anywhere. Breathe in through your nose for eight counts, hold your breath for four, and exhale through your mouth for seven. Slowing down your breathing sends a message to your brain to relax.

- **Cupcake Breaths**: Imagine you have a cake or cupcake with a candle in front of you. Try to blow out the candle slowly. This makes you breathe out gently and helps you calm down.

- **Blowing Bubbles:** You may feel like a little kid, but blowing bubbles from a bubble wand is a great way to practice breathing. The act of blowing bubbles forces the breath to come out slowly, which can decrease anxiety and stress.

Mindfulness Techniques

Mindfulness is the simple practice of bringing a gentle, accepting attitude to the present moment.

- **Engage Your Five Senses:** This simple exercise can distract you from complex emotions and help you focus on the present.

  ☞ Right now, I see...

☞ Right now, I hear...

☞ Right now, I am touching...

☞ Right now, I smell...

☞ Right now, I feel...

- **Mindful Listening:** Sit quietly with your eyes closed and listen to everything around you for a few minutes.

- **Perform a Body Scan:** Starting at your head or your toes, slowly scan your entire body, notice where you're holding tension, and try to release it.

- **Listen to a Meditation:** Apps like Calm and Headspace have meditations for kids and teens that target specific emotions. You can also find meditations on YouTube.

- **Do Yoga:** Yoga releases tension and stress from your body and mind.

- **Focus on a Mindful Word:**

    ☞ Think of a word that creates calm images, like waves, sunlight, or peace.

    ☞ Think about the word, saying it silently as you breathe in and out. Stay focused on the word.

    ☞ If/when your mind wanders, gently bring it back to your word.

    ☞ Continue for one to five minutes.

Personal Coping Strategies Toolkit for Emotional Regulation

Chapters three and four were full of ideas, tips, and strategies for regulating emotions and processing big or complex emotions. Not every method will work for everyone, so building a personal toolkit with strategies that work for you is important.

1. **Experiment with Different Strategies:** Try various tips to see which fits you best.

2. **Track What Works (and What Doesn't):** Keep a list of strategies you've tried, noting which helped and which didn't make much difference.

3. **Identify Your Emotional Triggers:** Pay attention to the situations that often require you to use emotional regulation tools. It could be before an exam, during sports events, at social gatherings, or when you're speaking in public.

4. **Find a Creative Outlet:** Choose a creative activity, like writing, drawing, playing music, or dancing to express your feelings. Remember, you don't have to share your creations with anyone unless you want to.

5. **Talk to Trusted People:** Build a support network of people you can open up to, such as teachers, friends, family members, or mentors.

6. **Prioritize Self-Care and Hobbies:** Allocate time for activities that bring you joy and relaxation. Engaging in hobbies and self-care practices is crucial for emotional well-being.

7. **Incorporate Relaxation Techniques:** Make sure your toolkit includes relaxation methods, like yoga, meditation, or breathing exercises. Find what helps you unwind and make it a regular part of your routine.

REMEMBER!

Difficult emotions are not fun, but they need to be handled and processed to prevent resentment, anger, and other uncomfortable emotions from building up and bubbling over. To manage difficult emotions, it is important to find ways to express yourself and distract your mind when needed. Find people you can talk to, hobbies you enjoy, and breathing or mindfulness techniques to help you relax and calm down.

5

BUILDING RESILIENCE
AND SELF-ESTEEM

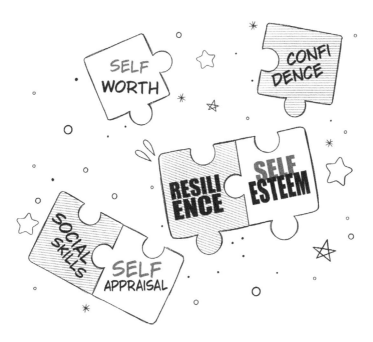

Resilience and self-esteem are two essential pieces of the puzzle that make you who you are! There are a lot of parts to your personality, but your self-esteem is one of the most crucial pieces. It is the center of who you are and how you feel about yourself. It's your overall sense of value or worth, and a measurement of how much you like, appreciate, and value yourself. [27]

Your self-esteem can change based on different factors, like how you're feeling physically, where you are, what you're doing, and who you're with. For instance, you might feel super confident and valued on the soccer field because you're a great player, and your self-esteem is likely high in that setting.

But if science isn't your strong suit, you might feel less confident in the chemistry lab, especially if it takes you longer to grasp new concepts, or if you have to ask for help more often than your classmates.

It is important to understand that not being a chemistry whiz doesn't make you any less valuable as a person — it just means the lab isn't where your strengths lie. Remember, your value doesn't decrease because of your challenges in certain areas.

---

27   *What Is Self-Esteem? A Psychologist Explains (positivepsychology.com)*

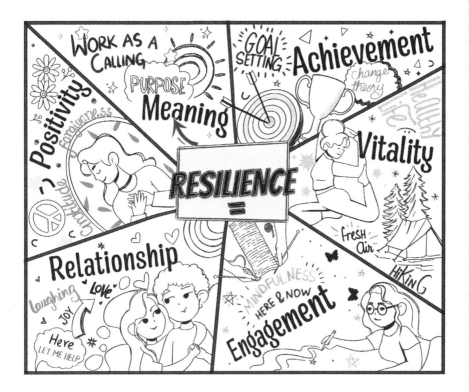

This is where resilience comes into play. According to the American Psychological Association, resilience is "the process and outcome of successfully adapting to difficult or challenging life experiences, especially through mental, emotional, and behavioral flexibility and adjustment to external and internal demands."[28]

Put simply, resilience is the ability to keep trying and going, even when things are tough. It is the ability to push your body and mind

28 Resilience (apa.org)

further and say, "It's OK that I am not the best at chemistry; I will still do my best and give it my all."

When you hit a tough spot, try asking yourself a few questions:

- Why is this getting to me?
- What can I do differently?
- Who can I ask for help?
- What small goals can I set for myself?
- How can I use what I'm good at to help me through?

Everybody has resilience, but if you don't practice it, it will become like a muscle that is never exercised: weak and ineffective. To strengthen your resilience, you need to use it repeatedly when facing challenges that threaten to knock your self-esteem.

So, how do you boost your self-esteem? Can you just say, "I've got this?" and move forward? In some cases, yes — but sometimes you might need to use a few more strategies.

Boosting Self-Esteem and the Importance of Resilience

Humans are emotional creatures that respond to people and situations. We're also affected by physical conditions like hunger levels, the amount of sleep we get, and even the weather. Because of this, our self-esteem and resilience can change from day to day.

For example, imagine it's the day of your gymnastics meet. If you slept well, enjoyed a nutritious breakfast, and received encouraging words from your best friend, you will likely feel confident.

But, if you were too anxious to sleep, woke up late, rushed your breakfast, and had a disagreement with your mom, your self-esteem might take a hit.

However, your gymnastic skills haven't changed. You've practiced just as much, and your body knows what to do. This is when resilience needs to kick in and crank up your self-esteem, allowing you to feel confident and perform your best, no matter the circumstances.

Why Building Your Resilience Matters: [29], [30]

- Resilience helps you rebound from setbacks or challenges, such as failing a test, missing the winning shot, or going through a breakup.

- Resilience helps you process and overcome challenges.

- Resilience can help you tap into your strengths, reach out to your support systems, and work through problems.

- Resilience helps you move forward, even when things don't work out as planned. It's the inner strength to carry on, even if you forget your lines in a play.

- Resilience allows you to learn and grow from failure and be less fearful of future challenges.

Tips to Boost Your Self-Esteem

- **Focus on Your Strengths:** Reminding yourself what you're good at can boost your confidence.

- **Get Physical:** Physical activity improves our mood and energy levels, which can improve your self-esteem.

29 What Is Resilience? Your Guide to Facing Life's Challenges, Adversities, and Crises (everydayhealth.com)

30 Resilience: Build skills to endure hardship — Mayo Clinic

- **Meditation and Mindfulness:** Meditation and mindfulness activities help you calm and center your feelings, making sense of why you feel a particular way. Being calm can help you feel more confident and self-assured.

- **Avoid Negative Influences:** If you have friends or even adults in your life who are negative influences, try to avoid them as much as possible. Avoid people who tease you, put you down, and make you feel small or unimportant. Surround yourself with people who support you!

- **Find a Hobby You Love:** Engaging in a beloved hobby or activity will make you feel good about yourself. Not only are you doing something you enjoy and are probably skilled at, you're also spending time with people who enjoy the same thing!

Developing Resilience: How to Build Resilience to Face Emotional Life Challenges

Now that you understand why resilience is important, let's discuss how to develop the skill.

Resilience builds over time, like muscles getting stronger the more you use them. Just as certain actions can build your resilience, others might wear it down. Tanya Kowalenko, an educator and writer, likens resilience to a bank account. The more positive actions or "deposits" you make into this account, the greater your resilience becomes. [31]

How do you fill up your resilience account and keep it topped up? Here are a few tips.

Tips for Building Resilience

- **Practice Gratitude**: Remembering what you're grateful for will make you feel stronger and more positive.

- **Volunteer**: Helping others gives you perspective on other people's lives (empathy) and makes you feel good.

- **Consider How You've Overcome Challenges in the Past**: What has worked before, and can you apply it to a new situation? For example, did breathing exercises calm you down before taking a big test? Maybe they'll also work before the homecoming dance.

- **Do Something Nice for Someone Else**: Similar to volunteering, helping others makes us feel good about ourselves and our abilities.

---

31 *Building Resilience — CMHA Haliburton, Kawartha, Pine Ridge (cmhahkpr.ca)*

- **Practice Mindfulness**: Mindfulness keeps popping up because it is an excellent tool for connecting with your inner thoughts and feelings.

- **Reframe Negative Thoughts**: Instead of saying, "There's no way I am going to finish this assignment on time," say, "I am going to do the best I can with the time available, and then I will talk to the teacher tomorrow if needed."

- **Have Fun**: Having fun boosts your energy, improves your mood, and makes you feel good in general, making you more resilient.

- **Spend Time with People You Care About**: Spending time with people who make you feel good about yourself is a guaranteed way to fill up your resilience account.

- **Get out into Nature**: Go for a walk, bike ride, or sit outside with a book.

Learning from Failures and Overcoming Emotional Challenges

Learning from failures and overcoming emotional hurdles are essential reasons why building resilience is so important. Facing failure is hard — it can leave you feeling embarrassed, disappointed, sad, or even angry, especially when you've invested a lot of effort. However, failure and disappointment are part of life, and everyone experiences them at some point.

Here are five incredible examples of people who failed numerous times before finding success: [32]

1. **Walt Disney** had his share of failures before creating his animation studio. Did you know he was fired from an early newspaper writing job for lacking creativity?

2. **J.K. Rowling** submitted "Harry Potter and the Sorcerer's Stone" to 12 publishers, all of which rejected her book. They said no one would want to read a story about a boy at a magical boarding school. They were wrong, of course!

3. **Bill Gates** dropped out of college and faced numerous failures before creating Microsoft, the largest computer company in the world.

4. **Michael Jordan** didn't make it onto his high school basketball team, and missed many crucial shots as a young player, but he became one of the greatest basketball players of all time.

5. **Abraham Lincoln** lost countless elections and suffered several personal tragedies, but he persevered and is well-known as one of the most influential American presidents.

Imagine how different the world would be if any of these five people gave up after their first, second, or third failures! Instead, each took

---

32 *55 Famous Failures Who Became Successful People (developgoodhabits.com)*

what they learned from their failures, adapted, made changes, and tried again. That is resilience in action.

Think of something you've recently struggled with. Did you try once and give up? Maybe you tried two or three times before you quit. Why did you decide to quit? Was it because it was too hard, or because you lost interest?

If something doesn't interest you, there might not be a reason to keep trying. But if it is something you enjoy or are determined to accomplish, keep going.

1. **Talk to someone knowledgeable in the area**. What insight can they provide?

2. **Do some research**. Read about it, watch how-to videos, or listen to interviews with people who have accomplished what you're trying to do.

3. **Decide why it is important to you**. Perhaps it is a matter of passing the next test so you don't fail the class, or maybe it's your dream to sing on a stage like "American Idol." Your motivations play a big role in how resilient you are in a situation.

What Does Failure Teach You? [33]

- **Resilience:** The ability to keep trying.

- **Humility:** The understanding that you can't be perfect or the best at everything, and that to fail is human.

- **Flexibility:** Learning how to grow, change, and try something different.

- **Creativity:** Learning to think outside the box, create new ideas, and find new ways of doing something.

- **Motivation:** The desire to keep trying. If everything were easy, we'd lose the motivation to try new things.

By learning from your failures and developing resilience, you are already on your way to boosting your confidence and improving your self-esteem. But there are other positive steps you can take to improve your self-perception.

---

33 *Why Learning from Failure Is Your Key to Success (betterup.com)*

Managing difficult emotions can feel uncomfortable, especially big feelings like jealousy, anger, or grief, but these uncomfortable emotions aren't necessarily bad. They need to be treated with care and support so you learn how to process them and move forward. Use your mistakes as learning opportunities to build resilience and self-esteem. Your strengths make you unique, and you can utilize them to process difficult emotions.

Techniques for Improving Self-Perception and Confidence

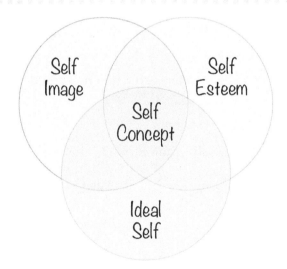

Self Image

Self Esteem

Self Concept

Ideal Self

Much of this chapter has covered self-esteem, but remember, self-esteem is just one part of your broader self-concept, or how you see yourself. Your self-concept is your overall view of yourself, answering the question "Who am I?"[34] It includes your self-image, ideal self, and self-esteem. Your self-concept might include aspects like:

- Gender: Female
- Age: 13
- Height: Tall
- Hair Color: Brown
- Roles: Big sister, daughter

- Hobbies: Piano player
- Religion: Jewish
- Nationality: American
- Personality: Friendly
- Appearance: Pretty

Your self-esteem reflects how much you value each of these traits and abilities. You might feel just okay about being female and wish for a slight boost in how you see this aspect of yourself. Yet, you might really cherish being a big sister, and feel proud and confident in this role!

For the same list, your self-esteem values may look like this:

- Female: Moderate
- Age 13: Low

- Tall: Low
- Brown Hair: Moderate

---

34 *What Is Self-Esteem? A Psychologist Explains (positivepsychology.com)*

- Big Sister: High
- Daughter: High
- Piano Player: Moderate
- Jewish: High

- American: Moderate
- Friendly: High
- Pretty: High

Self-concept can also be viewed as a circular system, with one factor constantly affecting the others.

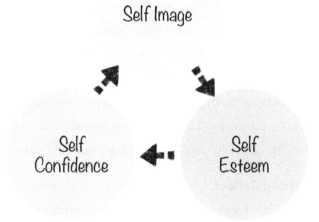

Because self-esteem and self-concept are linked, there are ways to boost one by strengthening the other:

- **Positive Self-Talk and Affirmations**: Positive self-talk can greatly boost your self-image. Tell yourself that you can score the goal, do the audition, or ace the test!

- **Practice Makes ~~Perfect~~ Improvement**: Remember, there is no such thing as perfect — but the more you practice a skill, the better you'll become. If you want to shine at the recital, practice your playing. If you want to become a better pitcher, get out there with a ball and pitch!

- **Listen to Others**: Other people will sometimes view us differently than we view ourselves. When it is people we trust, listening to their opinions and insights can help us. For example, your best friend may tell you that how you spoke to another classmate sounded mean and disrespectful. Maybe that wasn't your intention, but taking a moment to consider the interaction might help you get to know yourself better.

- **Journal and Reflect**: Using a journal to jot down your thoughts while they are fresh is helpful for understanding your motivations and feelings at a specific moment. A journal is something you can reference time and again when you need insight into your self-concept.

- **Recognize and Celebrate Your Strengths**: Everybody's good at something. Pat yourself on the back for everything you *can* do!

How to Recognize Your Strengths

To celebrate your strengths, you must first recognize them. Use the following activities to identify and appreciate your personal strengths and achievements:

1. **"I am…"**: Using a piece of paper and a pencil or pen, write as many positive "I am" statements as possible. For example, "I am a girl," "I am honest," "I am a good student," etc.

2. **Flip It**: Using 3x5 index cards, write out several recent mistakes, disappointments, or failures you've made or had. Now flip them over one at a time and turn them into positives. For example, one might read, "I didn't get the part I wanted in the musical." On side two, you could write, "I got a callback for the lead, and I was cast in the musical."

3. **Visualize Success**: Close your eyes and take a few minutes to imagine a situation where you've accomplished a goal. Use your five senses to describe what that feels, looks, sounds, tastes, and smells like. How did you accomplish this goal? What strengths did you utilize?

4. **Find Your Strengths**: Using the words in the boxes below, circle the ones that best reflect your strengths.

Wisdom	Artistic Ability	Curiosity	Leadership
Empathy	Honesty	Open Mindedness	Persistence
Enthusiasm	Kindness	Love	Social Awareness
Fairness	Bravery	Cooperation	Forgiveness
Modesty	Common Sense	Self-Control	Patience
Gratitude	Love of Learning	Humor	Spirituality
Ambition	Creativity	Confidence	Intelligence
Athleticism	Discipline	Assertiveness	Logic
Optimism	Independence	Flexibility	Adventurousness

NAVIGATING RELATIONSHIPS

"Communication is the lifeline of any relationship."
— Elizabeth Bourgeret

Understanding Emotional Dynamics

Emotional dynamics are all about how we react and interact with different people in our lives, and they play a big part in how we communicate. How you feel and act can change based on who you're with, where you are, and your mood before everything starts. But, no matter the situation, it's always possible to communicate in a kind and effective way. Let's look into some scenarios to see how emotional dynamics play out in real-life situations.

Scenario #1: A Stressful Morning

Imagine that you and your mom had a disagreement last night about your need to be more responsible. Today, you overslept because you forgot to set your alarm. Now, your mom is rushing you so she won't be late for work.

- The emotional dynamic between you and your mom is pretty tense. You're upset because you didn't live up to your promise to be more responsible, and she's frustrated about possibly being late. Mornings are usually hectic, but today feels extra stressful. Maybe you're a bit snappy or don't want to talk.

Scenario #2: A Day of Wins

Now picture a totally different day in which you aced your history test, your best friend lent you her favorite shirt, you got the first chair in the orchestra, and you scored in your soccer game. Plus, after school you're hanging out with your best friend at Starbucks.

· Your mood is way better. In fact, you're over the moon! Everything's going your way, and you're feeling excited and proud. You're all smiles, sharing your happiness with your best friend.

In both scenarios, the emotional dynamic was affected by who you were with, what happened, and how you felt about what was happening.

Now, take a look at a third scenario and decide what you think the emotional dynamic is.

Scenario #3: Anxious Excitement

Tonight, you're going out with friends, including your crush, who doesn't know you like them. You've decided tonight's the night you'll tell them, but you're in a bind: You can't find the jeans you wanted to wear, and your backup outfit doesn't match the shirt you picked out. To top it off, your best friend isn't replying to your texts for fashion advice.

Describe the emotional dynamic in the scene above:

Emotional dynamics will change from day to day, and sometimes from hour to hour. Thanks to puberty, as a tween or teen, you're going through a lot of changes. Hormones are reshuffling everything, including your feelings, changes in your body, your thoughts, and even how you interact with others. [35]

At this point, it's crucial to learn how to deal with the emotional ups and downs in different situations, whether with friends, family, acquaintances, or professional relationships.

Your relationships can be imagined as a set of circles around you.

---

35 *Understanding Emotion in Adolescents: A Review of Emotional Frequency, Intensity, Instability, and Clarity — Natasha H. Bailen, Lauren M. Green, Renee J. Thompson, 2019 (sagepub.com)*

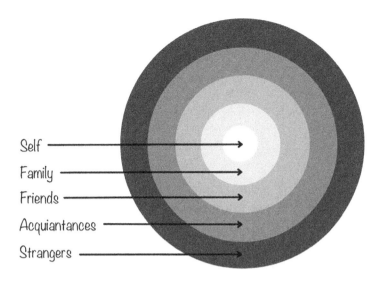

Self ——————————→

Family ——————————→

Friends ——————————→

Acquiantances ——————————→

Strangers ——————————→

In the middle is you. The next ring is your immediate or closest family members. The next one out is for close friends and relatives. Further out are the rest of your friends — maybe your teammates or church youth group members. Beyond that are acquaintances or people you are not close to emotionally, like your teachers, the barista you see daily, co-workers at your part-time job, and your school bus driver.

The way you feel and interact changes based on how close you are to someone and how you're feeling in the moment. Often, the most complex feelings come out when you are around the people you're closest to because that's where you feel safest being your true self.

Let's dive into the different levels of emotional dynamics and explore some tips for handling them effectively.

FRIENDSHIPS

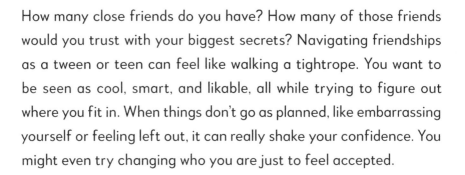

"Always love your friends from your heart not from your mood or need."

How many close friends do you have? How many of those friends would you trust with your biggest secrets? Navigating friendships as a tween or teen can feel like walking a tightrope. You want to be seen as cool, smart, and likable, all while trying to figure out where you fit in. When things don't go as planned, like embarrassing yourself or feeling left out, it can really shake your confidence. You might even try changing who you are just to feel accepted.

Remember, your true friends appreciate you for who you are. They will want to be friends with the true you. If you find yourself acting differently, dressing a certain way, or pretending to like things just to fit in, those people might not be your genuine friends.

Peer pressure is a big part of being a tween or teen. You might feel pushed to act in certain ways or make choices based on what your friends think is cool. But it's okay to stand up for what you believe is right, even if it means going against the crowd.

For example, imagine a scenario where a friend wants you to skip class, but you know it's a bad idea. You want to seem "cool," but you also don't want to disappoint your parents or miss out on learning. Or, maybe a new friend invites you to a party, but you've already committed to helping with a youth group event. Choosing between disappointing a friend and missing out on something fun can be tough.

How do you deal with these challenging situations? How do you stay true to yourself and keep your friendships and values intact? Sometimes, you might be able to find a balance; other times, you might need to think hard about what those friendships mean to you. Staying true to yourself is key, even when it's not the easiest decision.

Questions to Ask Yourself

- Think about the emotional dynamic of the friendship. Is this friendship a healthy choice? Do you feel good about yourself when you are with this friend? Is this friend there for you when you need them? Do you value this friendship?

- What are the possible outcomes of saying yes or no to a friend's request? What is the best and worst that could happen? How do you feel about those options?

- If a friend says or asks something of you that makes you feel uncomfortable or that you know is wrong, what would disagreeing with them look like? Would it ruin the friendship, or would they consider your opinion? If your disagreement ruins the friendship, it probably isn't a true friendship.

Additional Ideas to Consider [36],[37]

- Value honesty in your friendships. If you cannot be honest with your friends or they are not honest with you, that is a red flag.

- If you're struggling with a friend's opinion or suggestion, evaluate who they are. List their good qualities. Was this incident outside their normal behavior? Sometimes, people don't realize they said something offensive if they haven't been exposed to it before.

    ☞ Talk to them about why their opinion upset you using "I feel" statements. For example, "I felt sad when you said (blank), it was an unpleasant comment, and it hurt me," or "I felt disappointed when you used the term (blank). It's offensive, and that's not cool."

---

36   *7 ways to help your teen strengthen their friendships — ReachOut Parents*

37   *10 Tips To Help Your Teen Navigate Friendships (grownandflown.com)*

- Think of people you admire and want to emulate. Maybe your mom is a great friend and role model. Maybe there's a celebrity or professional athlete you look up to. What traits about them make them good people? You should seek those traits in your friendships and for yourself.

- Be the friend you want others to be to you.

- Ultimately, you can't change anyone who doesn't want to be changed. If a friend is exhibiting behaviors you don't like and you've discussed your feelings with them, it might be time to cut ties with them.

- Establish boundaries within your friendships and stick to them. For example, if a friend stands you up at Starbucks twice, you might decide not to make advance plans with them anymore. Or, if someone returns a borrowed shirt with a stain on it, you might tell them you won't share clothes with them again unless they can return items in good condition.

- Be able to forgive. Not every mistake needs to end a friendship. If a friend messes up, you can set a new boundary, but also forgive them. This gives them a chance to prove they're sorry, allowing both of you to move on together.

FAMILY

Many of these tips also apply to family relationships. You'll find that some family members, like your parents and siblings, are very close to you, while others, like aunts, uncles, cousins, and grandparents, might not be as close.

The big difference with family is that you don't get to choose them like you do your friends. However, you do have some say in how and when you interact with them, even though it might be limited. Family relationships can be complex, and it's up to you to figure out who you feel closest to and who might be more on the outskirts of your inner circle.

Tips on Talking to Your Parents

Tweens and teens often find talking to their parents challenging. There is a belief that your parents won't understand or listen to you. There is also the thought that parents don't know what it is like to be a kid today. In many ways, that is true.

Your parents likely grew up without smartphones, iPads, laptops, social media, or even Netflix! The way they hung out with friends and interacted with the world was very different. They might have had a family computer, and perhaps a laptop towards the end of college, but personal devices like smartphones likely weren't a part of their lives until much later.

Your parents couldn't share photos, thoughts, and memes via social media like we can today, and their actions weren't recorded and saved forever in a digital data bank.

It makes sense that your parents might not fully grasp the ins and outs of social media safety, usage, and protecting you online, which is ultimately what they want to do.

So, try your best to remember how different their teen years were when attempting to talk to them. Try some of these tips for effective communication:

- **Use "I feel" statements**. We've mentioned these a lot because they are a very effective form of communication that removes blame from the conversation. For example, "When you tell me I have to do my homework as soon as I get home, I feel overwhelmed and frustrated because I haven't had any time to relax or recover from the school day."

- **Be honest with your paren**ts. Trust must be earned! Lying to your parents about who you're with, what you're doing, and where you are will not help build your relationship.

- **Talk to your parents as often as you can**[38], even if it's just about simple stuff, like the weather, something you did at

---

38   *Talking to Your Parents or Other Adults (for Teens) | Nemours KidsHealth*

school, or a YouTube video you watched. The more you talk to your parents, the easier it will be.

- **Share your interests with them**. Your parents want to know what you like, but they may need to learn how to talk to you about it. Offer to teach them about Fortnite, fashion, or your favorite rapper.

- **For sensitive discussions, plan what you want to say to your parents ahead of time**. You can even practice it in front of a mirror.

- **Pick the right moment**. Starting a conversation about why you don't want to play violin anymore isn't ideal when your mom is busy getting your little brother ready for school.

Whether navigating friendships, family relationships, or more casual relationships, the keys to effective communication are using "I feel" statements, being calm and courteous, and being honest with your-self and the person you are speaking with.

However, despite our best efforts, conflicts can sometimes occur. When they do, there are some unique strategies you can use to calm things down and find a resolution.

Conflict Resolution Techniques

Whether you're disagreeing with your best friend over which dress to pick for the prom or having a heated discussion with your dad about getting a nose piercing, there are effective methods to calm tensions and resolve conflicts.

WHAT CAN I DO?

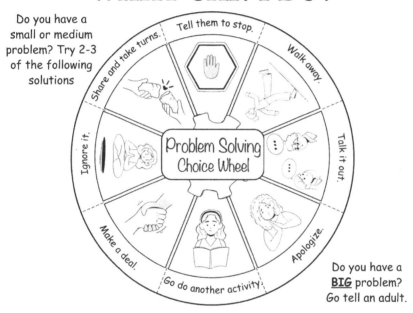

Do you have a small or medium problem? Try 2-3 of the following solutions

Share and take turns.

Tell them to stop.

Walk away.

Ignore it.

Problem Solving Choice Wheel

Talk it out.

Make a deal.

Go do another activity.

Apologize.

Do you have a **BIG** problem? Go tell an adult.

· **Take Turns:** Taking turns or sharing is a simple solution, especially with siblings or classmates. Suppose you're arguing every morning with your sister over who gets to use the bathroom, and when. Make a schedule and take turns. Each person has to agree to the schedule and then stick to it. It may not be ideal, but it is fair!

- **Tell the Person to Stop:** If someone is doing something inappropriate, hurtful, or that makes you uncomfortable, tell them to stop. You don't owe them an explanation. However, you can always use "I feel" statements to discuss why you told them to stop.

- **Talk About It:** Talking is a great way to solve conflicts. Find a safe space and allow each person to speak without interruption. Be sure to use "I feel" statements. When listening, don't think about what you want to say next. Truly listen to what the person is telling you.

- **Do Something Else:** If the conflict is minor and not worth arguing over, simply do something else. If you're fired up and angry and need space before you talk, doing something else is a great way to distract your mind and calm down before a discussion.

- **Apologize:** If you made a mistake, own it and apologize. Be sincere in your apology. Simply saying "I'm sorry" usually won't cut it, especially since it is overused.

- **Ignore It:** Is what happened simply not worth the time and effort to discuss? If so, then just ignore it. Maybe your brother accidentally grabbed your towel from the dryer, or your friend forgot the book she said you could borrow. These types of minor infractions don't need a big discussion, even if they're irritating.

- **Look at the Situation from Their Point of View**: In a conflict, it is easy to forget that the other person has opinions, feelings, and ideas, too. Try to look at the conflict from their side and use empathy to understand.

DEVELOPING EMPATHY

Empathy is a useful tool for navigating relationships and solving conflicts, and that's why it comes up so often. It is the ability to see a situation from another person's point of view, giving you a glimpse into their feelings and motivations. This understanding can guide how you react and what you do next.

Feeling empathy might be tough sometimes, like if your sibling breaks a prized possession of yours. But even a small amount of empathy can ease tension and help you handle the situation better.

Tips to Develop Empathy

- Build safe and secure relationships with your parents (or another trusted adult if your parents aren't an option). Research shows that teenagers with secure relationships with at least one adult are more empathetic to their peers and friends.

- Read about history and the struggles of different people throughout time. The more you know about the world you live in and how people got where they are, the more empathy you'll develop.

- Look at every situation from all possible points of view. The more expansive your understanding of a subject, the more empathy you will have for the other people involved. [39]

- Study art and photography. Art is a wonderful way to develop empathy, because you can look at a piece and try to imagine what the artist was feeling or what the picture represents. It is a good way to practice your empathy skills. [40]

---

39 *Help your teenager develop empathy — ReachOut Parents*

40 *5 Strategies for Teaching Empathy to Teens — Connections Academy*

Empathy Exercises

Want to practice and develop your empathy further? Try these empathy exercises:

- What's going on in this picture?

- ☞ Take a look at the photo above. Try to imagine the story behind it.
- ☞ What might the person be thinking or feeling? What do you think led up to the moment before the photo was taken?

- What does the following quote mean? How is it related to empathy?:

"If you look into someone's face long enough, eventually you're going to feel that you're looking at yourself."
— Paul Aster

· Fill out this empathy table.

EMPATHY

Empathy means seeing things from someone else's perspective rather than your own. Empathy helps you get along with others. It also helps you to build stronger relationships.

How can you practice empathy:

┌----------AT HOME?----------┐   ┌----------AT SCHOOL?----------┐
│   │   │   │
│   │   │   │
│   │   │   │
│   │   │   │
└----------------------------┘   └------------------------------┘

┌----WITH YOUR FRIENDS?----┐   ┌------WITH YOUR FAMILY?------┐
│   │   │   │
│   │   │   │
│   │   │   │
│   │   │   │
└--------------------------┘   └----------------------------┘

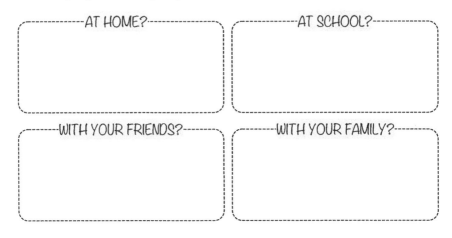

REMEMBER! Empathy is a powerful relationship tool. It helps you see a situation from another person's point of view, providing fresh insight you may have missed, which is useful when interacting with other people. When empathy alone isn't enough to navigate a relationship, there are conflict resolution techniques you can try to build stronger communication between you and your friends and family.

THE DIGITAL WORLD
AND EMOTIONS

Before starting this chapter, consider all the different ways you interact on social media. Do you have X (Twitter), Snapchat, or Discord? Do you watch videos on YouTube and TikTok? What about Instagram, Facebook, or Twitch?

The apps and sites mentioned are only some of the options teens use regularly. There are many more you might have tried or know about. According to data gathered in 2022, over half of U.S. teens use at least one social media platform, and 97% of teens use the Internet every day! [41]

YouTube, TikTok, Instagram, and Snapchat were the most visited sites among teens. Does that match your online activity? If so, are you aware of how to stay safe on these platforms? Do you know about the potential risks to your mental health and the impact of too much social media use or gaming on your brain?

Researchers across various fields, including science, psychology, and education, have been closely studying the effects of social media and digital technology on teens, especially focusing on mental health aspects. Their findings reveal a significant connection between social media use in teens and increased rates of depression and anxiety. [42]

---

[41] *Nearly half of US teens use the social media 'almost constantly' | World Economic Forum (weforum.org)*

[42] *Social media harms teens' mental health, mounting evidence shows. What now? (science-news.org)*

Given these findings, it's essential for you as a tween or teen to understand the impact that the digital world can have on your emotional well-being. It's equally important to know how to navigate the online space safely, ensuring you protect both your physical and mental health while using the Internet.

How the Digital World Affects and Influences Emotions

Digital technology is still relatively new. The Internet has only been around since 1969, and didn't become common in homes until the mid-1990s [43] — around the time your parents might have been your age. Social media is even more recent, but has rapidly become a significant part of our lives.

The Internet and digital technology have evolved quickly over the last 30+ years, but research into their effects on us is still in its early stages. However, findings so far are worrying, especially the links between social media usage and increased rates of depression and anxiety among teenagers.

Computers, smartphones, and digital technology are now a part of our everyday lives, making them hard to avoid completely. However,

---

43 *History of the Internet: Origin and Timeline — Tech Quintal*

becoming aware of their potential risks is the first step towards effectively managing and reducing screen time.

Social Media

Social media began in 1997, but didn't truly catch on until the launch of MySpace in 2004. This means social media has only been a part of our lives for about 20 years, making it a relatively young phenomenon.

Facebook, an early social media giant, started in 2004 as a platform for Harvard students, later expanding to other colleges and certain companies before opening to the general public in 2006. Today, it boasts over 3 billion registered users, with more than 2 billion active every day. [44]

Facebook usage among tweens and teens has declined, but you may use or have heard of WhatsApp or Instagram, which the company also owns. Platforms like Snapchat, launched in 2011, and TikTok (2018) have surged in popularity, particularly among tweens and teens. [45]

---

44 *Facebook User & Growth Statistics to Know in 2024 (backlinko.com)*

45 *The History of Facebook and How It Was Invented (thoughtco.com)*

A Pew Research Center study highlighted the fact that a significant portion of teens are almost constantly on social media, with You-Tube, TikTok, Instagram, and Snapchat the most popular. [46]

Think back to the question at the beginning of this chapter: How many different social media apps do you use? Are there any others not mentioned here that you use frequently?

Over half of the teens in the same study said it would be hard to give up social media. Is that number too high or too low? How would you feel if you had to give up social media for an hour, a day, or even a week?

DID YOU KNOW? According to a recent study, girls use social media more than boys — an average of 3.4 hours per day, compared to 2.1 hours per day for boys. [47] Girls also said it would be harder to give up than boys. [48]

---

46   *Teens, Social Media and Technology 2022 | Pew Research Center*

47   *Social media harms teens' mental health, mounting evidence shows. What now? (science-news.org)*

48   *Teens, Social Media and Technology 2022 | Pew Research Center*

The older the teens, the greater their dependence on social media. That's likely due to the addictive nature of social media.

Did you know that checking your favorite app and getting likes and comments triggers a dopamine release in your brain — the same chemical that makes us feel good? Every time you get a dopamine hit, your interest in using that app goes up, which means you keep going back for more.

Unfortunately, spending a lot of time on social media can lead to some negative situations: [49]

- Low self-esteem: Seeing everyone else's "perfect" lives online can incorrectly make you feel like yours isn't as good.

- Loneliness: Although social media connects people, it can also create feelings of isolation and loneliness.

- Poor school performance: Using screens too much can make it hard to focus on homework or studying, leading to poor grades.

- Depression and anxiety: Spending too much time on social media can make some people withdraw socially and feel down.

- Lack of empathy: Social media can make it harder to feel or express empathy face-to-face.

49   *Social Media Addiction: What It Is and What to Do About It (healthline.com)*

- FOMO (fear of missing out): Worrying about missing out can lead to even more social media usage. [50]

- Trouble sleeping: Using social media or screens right before bedtime can negatively affect sleep.

- Less exercise and physical activity: Time spent on screens tends not to be active, which may affect your overall health.

- Fewer real-world connections: While online friendships can be great, they don't quite meet the need for real-life connections with people close to you (friends, family, teammates, etc.).

Constantly comparing ourselves to others online can lower our self-esteem, change how we see ourselves, and make us worry about how we look to others.

INFLUENCERS

Influencers are a big part of why we might feel left out (FOMO) or compare our lives to others on social media.

Influencers only show the very best moments of their lives. They take lots of shots to get it right, use special lighting, and often have

---

50 *5 Ways Social Media Affects Kids' Mental Health (and How Parents Can Help!) — Family-Education*

brands giving them free stuff to show off. Remember, what many influencers show isn't real life.

Nonetheless, watching their perfect-looking lives on YouTube or Instagram can make you feel not good enough and hurt your self-esteem.

Sometimes, you might know the people you're talking to online, but other times (like when you're looking at influencers' posts), you don't know them at all. Talking to someone online without seeing their face is called faceless communication.

While talking to people without seeing them is common, it's not always clear, and can make you feel upset or misunderstood.

Faceless Communication

Most social media and digital communication is faceless, meaning you can't see the person you're interacting with. If you text with your friends you know and see regularly, you may not worry too much about this. However, if you interact with people you don't know on social media platforms, there is no guarantee that the person you're speaking with is who they say they are.

Pictures and profiles are constantly being faked, and with the increase of AI technology, it is even easier to fake photos.

REMEMBER!

The safest way to interact online is to ONLY accept friend requests from people you know.

If you do not know the person at the other end of the chat, never provide them your real name, age, address, photo, where you live or go to school, or any information they can use to identify who and where you are.

Never click on any links sent to you or open any attachments.

If a person's comments ever make you feel uncomfortable or are inappropriate, block the person and tell a trusted adult.

It's important to remember that faceless communication, even from people you know, can also negatively impact your emotional well-being.

Cyberbullying

Cyberbullying (bullying that happens over texting and social media) is a trend on social media, and one that parents and teachers often have trouble detecting.

What exactly is cyberbullying? According to stopbullying.gov, "Cyberbullying includes sending, posting, or sharing negative, harmful, false, or mean content about someone else. It can include sharing personal or private information about someone else, causing embarrassment or humiliation." [51]

If you're experiencing cyberbullying, it's really important to get help. Talk to an adult you trust about it as soon as you can.

Try not to reply or fight back. Instead, block the person causing you trouble and consider taking a break from social media and your phone. Before you delete any hurtful messages, make sure to take screenshots. This way, you'll have proof of what happened.

Also, report the person bullying you to the website or app where it's happening. The site's administrators might be able to stop the bully from using the platform.

DOWNSIDES OF FACELESS COMMUNICATION

Faceless communication, like texting or chatting online, misses out on a lot of important cues we get from talking in person. When we're face-to-face, we can see someone's expressions, hear the tone of

---

51   *What Is Cyberbullying | StopBullying.gov*

their voice, and notice their body language. Without these, it's easy to get confused or misunderstand each other.

Here are some problems that can come from communicating without seeing or hearing each other:

- **Arguments from Misunderstandings**.

- **Slow Response Time**: Sometimes, you need a quick answer, like knowing if you have a ride to soccer practice. Waiting for a text reply can be frustrating.

- **Saying Mean Things:** People might say things online they'd never say in person, especially if they're anonymous. They might feel more comfortable being mean or inappropriate without seeing the other person's reaction. It feels "safer" to hide behind a screen.

- **Feeling Disconnected:** It's tough to connect with someone emotionally if you can't see or hear them.

If you're finding it hard to connect with people because you're not seeing them in person, or if spending a lot of time online is making you feel down, there are ways to deal with these feelings and improve your emotional well-being.

Navigating Emotional Challenges Online

Dealing with the emotional ups and downs of online life can be tough. Here are some strategies to help you handle these challenges:

- **Take a Break:** Stepping away from social media can be really good for you. One study found that by simply reducing online time by 15 minutes per day for three months, people slept better, felt more positive, and got sick less often.[52]

- **Talk to Someone Real:** Find someone you trust to talk to in person, like a family member, teacher, or friend.

- **Don't React Immediately:** It's easy to react immediately when you see something upsetting online, but it's often better to wait. When you're emotional, you might not make the best choices.

- **Get Active:** Spending a lot of time on your phone or computer can mean you're not moving around much. Exercise can make you feel happier and healthier — plus, getting some sunshine is great, too!

- **Set Boundaries**: It's important to have rules for yourself about how you use social media:

  - ☞ Think about how long you should be online each day.
  - ☞ Decide who you will interact with online.

---

52 *Social Media Use and Poor Health | Psychology Today*

☞ Have a plan for what to do if someone makes you feel bad or says something that's not okay.

☞ Choose which websites or apps are good for you to visit.

Making these choices can help you feel better and keep your online life healthy.

Create a Digital Well-Being Plan

Creating a Digital Well-Being Plan is a smart way to manage how social media and digital interactions impact your mental and physical health. Here's how you can start:

Understand Your Usage

Think about and answer these questions:

- What role does social media play in your life? Is it crucial to you? If so, why?

- Are there any apps, websites, or games you feel you can't live without?

- Do you think you're spending too much time online? Explain your reasons.

 **Digital Wellbeing Worksheet**

Track Your Usage

Log your digital activities for a week:

- Note down how long you spend on each site or app. For example, if you play a game from 5:15 PM to 7:15 PM, that's two hours. If you're on Facebook from 3 PM to 3:30 PM, write down 30 minutes.

- Try to be as accurate as possible to understand your habits better.

Use tools to help:

- iPhone users can check their app usage in "Screen Time" under settings.

- Android users have "Digital Well-Being" in their settings to track app usage. You can also set limits for apps you use too much.

Reflect on Your Feelings

- Regularly note how you feel before and after using social media. Does your mood change? Do you feel happier, more stressed, or the same?

Adopt Good Habits

- Keep devices out of your bedroom at night and turn off electronics 30–45 minutes before bedtime. Use this time for non-screen activities.

- Try setting your screen to grayscale to reduce the rewarding feeling you get from colorful screens.

Setting Limits

- Consider setting a usage limit if you find you're using an app more than you'd like. Your phone can help by blocking access to the app once you've hit your daily limit.

By following these steps, you'll be well on your way to creating a balanced digital life that supports your emotional well-being and keeps you safe online.

REMEMBER! Using digital devices, particularly for social media, can impact your emotional well-being. But that doesn't mean you have to give them up completely. Take a realistic look at how and if social media and digital engagement affect you, and make a Digital Well-Being plan to stay healthy and connected with the world around you.

GROWING TOGETHER—
FAMILY ACTIVITIES

"Families are the compass that guides us. They are the inspiration to reach great heights and our comfort when we occasionally falter."
— Brad Henry

Our families are essential to our well-being and development. Every person on this planet has a family. Some are luckier than others and have families that love, support, and guide them. We hope that you are one of those people.

This chapter might be challenging to read if your family is not a place of comfort and support. But know that you can create your own group of people who care about you and support you by reaching out to other trusted adults, friends, and people within your community.

The Family's Role in Supporting Emotional Development

Parents are a child's first teachers. They taught you how to socialize, speak, and interact with others. They were crucial in your early emotional development, and they still have an important role to play in this regard. Did you know that, for young children, a mother's voice plays an essential role in their health and development, impacting their stress levels, social bonding, feeding skills, and speech processing? [53]

---

53 *How a mother's voice shapes her baby's developing brain | Britannica*

As you get older, your instinct might be to turn away from your parents when faced with an emotional challenge. A recent study showed that teens are biologically designed to tune out their mother's voices in favor of their peers. [54] Scientists believe these changes in brain development allow teens to develop healthy social skills among their friendship groups. But, even if you are biologically designed to tune out your parents, they are still an excellent source of guidance to help you develop emotionally.

Your parents and immediate family should be a place of comfort and safety. Your family is your base for exploring feelings and relationships. Families help guide you as you navigate experiences in different settings, including school, social settings, or your first job.

Your family teaches you about values, culture, social norms and behaviors, responsibility, and independence. For example, you may have learned from your family that stealing is wrong, showing respect to older people is expected, or that you should take your shoes off when you enter a house.

You may have family rituals and customs centered around specific holidays, roles, and religious ceremonies. You might have learned to respect hard work and care for those less fortunate than you.

---

54   *New Study Reveals the Reason Teens Seem to Tune Out Their Mom's Voice : ScienceAlert*

These learned skills and scenarios have developed who you are and shaped your social-emotional development — but your family's job isn't done yet!

As a tween, your family is a valuable resource for shaping how you interact with and perceive the world.

Activities to Foster Family Bonding and Emotional Engagement

Ever since birth or adoption, you have been building an emotional bond with your family. As a baby, your bond started with feedings, diaper changes, playtime, and your parents talking and interacting with you.

That bond has continued to grow and deepen throughout your life as your family has become a source of comfort, safety, and trust. As a tween, you might start questioning your role in the world and within your family, and struggle to figure out where you belong. This is normal, and you're not alone in asking these questions.

Research has shown that children develop vital social skills and higher self-esteem when families enjoy activities together. Daily activities, specially planned activities, and games are great ways to foster the bond between you and your family.

Daily Activities That Foster Emotional Development

There are a number of everyday activities you can adopt to develop your emotional development and create deeper bonds with your family, including:

- **Carpooling:** Asking your parents to help you carpool with friends to school, sports events, church, etc., teaches you about responsibility, problem-solving, and teamwork. You are sharing the responsibility of arriving on time with your peers, and teamwork is required to ensure everyone arrives on time.

- **Family Meals:** Eating meals as a family is a powerful bonding opportunity. Family meals provide a sense of security and belonging. While it's not always possible every day, try to find a few nights per week to sit and eat together.

- **Scheduling Time Together**: Make time with your family for a scheduled event. Ask your parents to go to the mall or the movies together. Go to a sports event or visit a museum in the city. Your parents might not realize that you, as a tween, want to spend time with them! Make an effort and ask *them* to hang out.

- **Choosing Family over Friends:** As a tween, the urge to hang with your friends is strong, but sometimes family needs to come first. Choosing special family events, rather than your friends, boosts your empathy, responsibility, and emotional management.

- **Earning an Allowance:** If your parents don't provide an allowance, discuss the possibility of earning one in exchange for work and chores around the house. Working for your allowance teaches you financial responsibility and the importance of self-discipline and hard work.

- **Volunteering Together**: Volunteering as a family is an excellent way to bond and build empathy. The more we give and help others, the more grateful we feel about our lives. Sharing these emotional experiences with your family can strengthen your bond. [55]

GAMES AND ACTIVITIES TO FOSTER FAMILY BONDING

In addition to daily or routine activities, you can play games and activities as a family specifically designed to strengthen the family unit. These include:

- **Family Game Night:** Game nights are a fun way for your family to bond. Family members can take turns choosing the game, or you can play games on a rotation. Playing games with your family provides a shared experience and a sense of unity and bonding. Plus, it gives the winner bragging rights for the week!

---

55   *How to Strengthen Family Bonds (verywellfamily.com)*

- **Team Sports:** If your family is active, turn family game night into team sports. You could play two-on-two basketball in your backyard, go bowling, or play minigolf. Remember, it's not so much about winning but about spending time together.

- **Role-Playing Games:** Role-playing is a great way to practice new behaviors and skills. For example, if one family member struggles with expressing their emotions, a role-playing game might help. This could include games like charades, where you practice acting out emotions or switch roles with your parents and pretend to be the adult.

- **Emotions Ball**: This activity is perfect for kids who struggle with or are uncomfortable expressing their feelings through words. You'll need a permanent marker and a beach ball. On each colored section of the ball, write down different emotions, such as anger, happiness, anxiety, etc. Sit in a circle with your family and pass the ball around. Whoever catches the ball should share a personal experience or moment when they felt the emotion written on the section facing them on the ball. [56]

- **Family Meetings**: Family meetings can be an excellent time to check in and openly discuss concerns or future plans. For instance, a family meeting might be the perfect time to discuss

---

56 *10 Family Therapy Activities for Building Relationships (healingcollectivetherapy.com)*

changes to your family chore rotation, or more exciting things like vacations, holiday plans, or a family outing. [57]

- **Miracle Question:** This exercise encourages family members to imagine a future where their problems are miraculously solved. Each family member describes what their life would be like if, overnight, any issues they might have disappeared. This exercise helps family members share problems, goals, and desires. It creates opportunities to openly discuss the steps needed to move closer to that ideal future. [58]

Discussion Guide to Enhance Emotional Discussions Between Parents and Tweens

Talking with your parents about big emotional issues and concerns might be challenging for you right now. It might feel awkward, uncomfortable, or even embarrassing, especially if you don't typically talk to your parents about sensitive or personal topics. You might not realize it, but your parents aren't always 100% sure what to say to you, either! They may feel uncomfortable, embarrassed, or awkward!

The more you talk to your parents, even about the simple and easy stuff, the easier it will be to open up about the big stuff. If you're

---

57   *How to Strengthen Family Bonds (verywellfamily.com)*

58   *10 Family Therapy Activities For Building Relationships (healingcollectivetherapy.com)*

struggling with talking to your parents and need tips to start conversations, here are some discussion guide ideas and questions to enhance emotional discussions.

You could turn these questions into a game or activity by writing prompts on slips of paper and choosing one at random to answer.

Personal Questions:

1. What is something you like about yourself?
2. What is one of your earliest memories?
3. What's one of your favorite memories?
4. What are things you're working on improving? How are you doing that?
5. What do you like to do for fun?
6. When do you feel happiest?
7. What helps you feel better when you're upset or stressed?
8. When have you felt angry recently?
9. When are some times you've felt worried recently?
10. What do you do to cope with your feelings?
11. What is something you're looking forward to?
12. What are you most proud of this past year?
13. What's the best compliment you've ever had?
14. What does your perfect day look like?
15. If you could be famous, would you? What would you want to be famous for?

Family & Friends

1. What are our family values?
2. What are our most important family traditions?
3. What do you like most about me/your other parent/siblings?
4. What would you change about me?
5. What do you think I like most about you?
6. What do you think I would change about you?
7. What is something you wish I would do more often?
8. Do you feel comfortable talking to me about anything?
9. Is there anything you wish our family would do together more often?
10. Do you think the discipline in our family is fair? What would you change?
11. Who are your closest friends now?
12. What do you enjoy doing with your friends?
13. Have your friendships changed in the past year? How? Why?
14. What do you look for in a friend?
15. How do you know if someone is not your friend?

Current Events/Culture

1. What are your favorite shows? Why?
2. What is an event that you heard about recently that concerns you? Why?
3. What social media platforms do you use? What do you like about that platform?

4. What are some positive things you've experienced about social media?
5. If you could travel anywhere in the world, where would you go?
6. What is your biggest goal in life?
7. What do you hope your life will be like 10 years from now?
8. If you had $100,000 to spend, how would you spend it?
9. Would you ever get a tattoo? Why or why not? What would it be?
10. What are the things that my generation doesn't understand about your generation?

REMEMBER!

Your family should be a source of support and comfort. If they're not a safe place, you can find other adults you trust, like teachers, coaches, or other relatives, who you can use as a source of stability. Talking to your parents isn't always easy, but they're probably unsure how to talk to you, too. If you struggle to talk to your parents, use a conversation starter or find a common interest you can share with them. The more you talk to your parents and work on developing your bond, the easier communication will become and the stronger your bond will be.

YOUR EMOTIONS, YOUR CREATIVITY

"Every artist dips his brush in his own soul, and paints his own nature into his pictures."
—Henry Ward Beecher

Art and creativity are closely tied to emotions.

When actors play different characters, they portray the characters' feelings to make us believe them. When songwriters write songs, they tell stories or express their feelings through words. When artists paint a peaceful beach or a bustling city, they put their feelings and experiences onto the canvas.

Creativity is a great way to express your emotions. For instance, you may listen to different songs when happy, sad, anxious, or angry.

Writers create poems about all sorts of feelings, including love, hatred, and jealousy. Artists have captured scenes of love, destruction, serenity, and wonder. Dancers use their bodies to express passion, joy, and sadness.

Do you have a preferred way to express yourself creatively? Do you sing, draw, write, knit, or play a musical instrument? Or do you find engaging with creativity a healthy way to process emotions? Perhaps you like to listen to music, watch movies, or visit art museums.

There is no wrong way to express yourself creatively, as long as it is healthy and not harmful or offensive to others.

Take a few moments to draw or color how you're feeling right now in the frame below. It can be scribbles and swirls, stick figures, or a detailed picture.

How did drawing your emotions feel? Did you enjoy it? Were you surprised by any of the emotions? If you liked this activity, you can do it whenever you feel the need to express your emotions creatively. All you need is blank paper and something to color or draw with!

Even if you don't consider yourself a creative or artsy person, there is probably some form of art you connect with. It's just a matter of finding it.

In addition to being a healthy way to express your emotions, creativity has many other benefits for your body, brain, and well-being.

The Benefits of Creative Emotional Expression

> *"Creativity is intelligence having fun"*
> -Albert Einstein

There are many great quotes about creativity, but the one above by Albert Einstein is simple yet true. To be creative, you must also have intelligence.

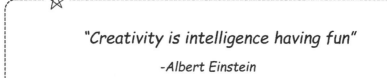

DID YOU KNOW? Animals also exhibit creativity and problem-solving skills. Their creative behaviors often lead to survival advantages, demonstrating creativity's importance beyond just art and culture.

Creativity isn't just about making art — it also helps us solve problems, handle complex emotions, and find comfort or purpose. It also offers a method of self-discovery, self-expression, and emotional release, combating uncomfortable emotions and helping us reframe our thoughts. [59]

Through creativity, we get to know ourselves better, express our feelings, and sometimes shift our moods by simply doing something different.

When you're creative, you step out of your daily routine. It makes your brain focus on something new, which can be a refreshing break from whatever is bothering you.

Creativity also breaks you free from your routine and forces your brain to think and focus on something other than your emotions. Sometimes, this break is enough to lighten your mood and help you refocus. [60]

All forms of creative expression are beneficial, but different types of creativity may offer different kinds of relief.

Music

Creative expression through music includes everything from playing an instrument or singing to dancing or listening to music. These

59 What Is Creativity? Top 5 Mental Health Benefits (mind.help)

60 How Creativity Positively Impacts Your Health (verywellmind.com)

different types of emotional expression benefit your body and brain in many different ways, including:

- **Making You Feel Good**: Physical activities like dancing release dopamine and serotonin. These feel-good hormones lift your mood and foster happiness. [61]

- **Helping Reduce Stress**: Dancing helps reduce stress levels.

- **Social Bonding**: Singing in a choir or group or making music with others creates positive feelings toward those people by producing oxytocin, which helps with social bonding. [62]

- **Building Trust**: Listening to music also releases oxytocin and builds our ability to trust others.

WRITING

Writing takes many forms. It can be storytelling, poetry, song lyrics, letters, or journaling. Writing is a healthy way to express emotions in a safe and private space. Nothing you write ever has to be shared with anyone else, but it can provide a great outlet to process uncomfortable emotions or difficult events. In short, writing is great. Its benefits include:

---

61   *Working out boosts brain health (apa.org)*

62   *How Creativity Positively Impacts Your Health (verywellmind.com)*

- **Stimulating the Brain:** Writing stimulates the mind, improving cognitive function and enhancing mental abilities. [63]

- **Developing Creativity and Imagination:** Storytelling involves imagination and creativity, and provides an outlet for expressing emotions in make-believe settings.

- **Thought Processing:** Writing about your emotions forces you to slow down and organize your thoughts. Through the writing process, you will learn how to recognize and regulate your emotions better. [64]

ART

Have you ever looked at a painting and been drawn into the picture or setting? Art is naturally emotive. This means that you automatically feel something when you look at a piece of artwork. Of course, you might not always like what you see, but it will usually trigger an emotion. You might find it calming or upsetting. It might make you happy or sad. When you interact with art, you often imagine another person's feelings and point of view, and when you create art of your own, it can be an avenue to release your own feelings. Art's benefits also include:

---

63 *What Is Creativity? Top 5 Mental Health Benefits (mind.help)*

64 *Writing about emotions may ease stress and trauma — Harvard Health*

- **Helps Develop Empathy:** Interacting with art, especially from other cultures, develops empathy. [65]

- **Helps Relieve Stress:** Drawing and painting relieve stress. [66]

- **Boosts Brain Functioning:** Painting and drawing strengthen the brain, increasing cognitive function. [67]

- **Increases Memory:** Engaging in art increases memory. [68]

- **Builds Patience:** Creating art teaches you patience, and that mistakes and re-starts are OK. Without making mistakes, you'll never figure out what works best and why! [69]

OTHER CREATIVE EXPRESSIONS

Beyond your typical forms of creative expression, like music, dancing, art, and writing, there are other ways to express your emotions creatively and improve your overall emotional mindset and coping skills. These include:

- **Puzzles** improve cognitive function and stimulate the brain. Whether you like traditional jigsaw puzzles, LEGO kits, crosswords, or sudoku, they all positively affect your brain.

---

65   *Children and Art: Creativity, Empathy, and Cultural Awareness (kneebouncers.com)*

66   *How Creativity Positively Impacts Your Health (verywellmind.com)*

67   *What Is Creativity? Top 5 Mental Health Benefits (mind.help)*

68   *How Creativity Positively Impacts Your Health (verywellmind.com)*

69   *Why being creative is good for you (bbc.com)*

- **Cooking** gives you a space to be creative and provides a sense of accomplishment. It teaches patience and can improve your relationship with food. Cooking also gives you an opportunity to care for and connect with others. [70]

- **Gardening** teaches you how to care for other living things. Plus, being outside and interacting with nature has been proven to improve your mood.

- **Knitting, crocheting, and sewing** are all relaxing, and another way to express yourself creatively. Consider making items to donate to those in need, as helping others also helps improve your mood.

- **Playing board games** teaches many life skills, including communicating with others, problem-solving, and developing self-confidence. [71]

Where to Start: Creative Projects to Explore Emotional Experiences

Starting a new project or learning new skills might feel scary. You might worry you won't be good at it, or that you will embarrass yourself. However, your form of creativity is neither good nor bad, because every person sees things differently. How you view the

---

70   *7 Ways Cooking Can Boost Your Mental Health (livekindly.com)*

71   *How Creativity Positively Impacts Your Health (verywellmind.com)*

world is very different from how anyone else sees the world, so all you have to do is start! Pick one of the projects below that interests you, and give it a try. Then, come back and try another one.

Journal about your experiences and the emotions you explore through the process as another way of monitoring how your emotions ebb and flow.

DANCE

There are many different ways to dance, including tap, salsa, ballet, hip-hop, modern, and Irish step dance. If you're not interested in taking formal dance classes, look for dance tutorials online.

YouTube has almost every dance style you can imagine for viewing and learning. You can practice in the privacy of your room, and no one will judge you because no one can see.

If you're not interested in formal dance, anytime you feel a big, uncomfortable emotion, put on some music and just move. Don't worry about how you're moving — simply let it all out!

ADULT COLORING BOOKS

If you think coloring books are only for little kids, then you're wrong! There is an entire market for adult coloring books. Adult coloring books are more intricate and detailed than your standard Mickey Mouse or Peppa Pig books. Using adult coloring books has been proven to be relaxing, improve brain function, reduce anxiety and stress, and improve your sleep. [72]

Because adult coloring pages have much more detail than a children's coloring book, they take longer to complete a page. This gives you a project to focus on and provides a sense of accomplishment and completion when you are done, much like finishing a big puzzle.

MURALS AND MOSAICS

Murals and mosaics are two styles of artwork that require creativity and patience. A mural is a large painting that usually goes on the side of a building. You often find them in cities or large towns. Mosaics combine tiny pieces of stone, gems, glass, etc., to create a picture.

Both of these types of projects require planning and strategy. You have to plan what you want, how you will create it, and what materials you will use, and use time management to complete it.

Through the process of planning the project, you'll explore many emotions. You can use the project to work through any uncomfortable or challenging emotions or experiences you are going through.

---

72   Interested in Coloring? 7 Benefits of Coloring for Adults (webmd.com)

Don't worry if you don't have a wall available. You can also paint a mural on a large piece of wood or a series of canvases.

WRITE A STORY

Writing a story is an incredibly beneficial way to express your emotions creatively. Like your art or your dance, no one has to see it or read it if you don't want them to, but it still provides an outlet to pour all your feelings onto paper.

DID YOU KNOW?

Many famous writers and poets dealt with depression, anxiety, and other mental illnesses.[73,74] They found writing to be highly therapeutic:

- Ernest Hemingway
- F. Scott Fitzgerald
- Sylvia Play
- Emily Dickinson
- Virginia Woolf
- Edgar Allan Poe
- Charles Dickens

---

73   7 Famous Writers Who Lived with Mental Illness — H2H
     (halfway2hannah.com)

74   The 10 Most Famous Writers Who Suffered With Mental Illnesses —
     whatNerd

Activity: Emotional Art Project to Visually Express Feelings

If you need a way to express your feelings visually but don't know what to do or don't have the time for a big project like the ones already listed, try one of these emotional art activities.

 **Creative Project Worksheets x3**

· Wordplay Association Worksheet

· Art Sequence Worksheet

· Words to Live by Collage Worksheet

REMEMBER!

Emotions and creativity are linked and can inspire each other. Use your creativity to channel uncomfortable or big emotions you're struggling to process or need more time to sit with. But remember, creativity isn't only for feelings we think of as negative. We can also express positivity and joy! Use dance, music, art, writing, or whatever creative outlet speaks to you the most, and try your hand at expressing your emotions creatively.

10

LOOKING AHEAD — BUILDING YOUR EMOTIONAL FUTURE

"Emotional self-awareness is the building block of the next funda-mental emotional intelligence: being able to shake off a bad mood."
— Daniel Goleman

As American psychologist Daniel Goleman said, emotional self-awareness is the building block of emotional intelligence. To grow emotionally, you have to be aware of your emotions and know how to manage them. Put simply, it is important to be able to shake off a bad mood.

It sounds simple, but controlling your emotions, especially as a tween or teen, can be complicated. Fortunately, it's not impossi-ble. Creating an emotional growth plan, developing a strategy, and working toward short- and long-term goals are building blocks you can put in place to secure a healthy emotional future.

You may not be worried about your emotional health or future emo-tional well-being right now. You might have more important things to worry about, like your science test, making the softball team, and who is going to the homecoming dance with whom. Those are all valid and realistic concerns and thoughts for someone your age.

But what happens if you fail the science test, you make the softball team but your best friend doesn't, and the person you hoped would ask you to the homecoming dance is going with someone else? Do you have the tools to handle those situations and emotions?

The more you practice emotional growth and strategies, the easier it will become. Then, when you are older and have other adult-sized situations and emotions, you'll be prepared to handle whatever comes your way.

Preparing for Your Emotional Future

What does preparing for your emotional future even look like? It starts with a five-step process[75], some of which you've already done by reading this book and completing the exercises.

1. Assess Your Emotional Intelligence Level
2. Set Realistic and Meaningful Goals
3. Daily Practice of Emotional Intelligence Skills
4. Learn and Grow from Your Mistakes
5. Celebrate Your Successes and Progress

Let's examine each of the five steps in more detail.

Assess Your Emotional Intelligence Level

If you want to grow emotionally, you need somewhere to grow from — a baseline. Throughout this book, there are exercises and activities designed to help you assess and work on your emotional intelligence. *Chapter Two: Exploring Your Emotions* has quite a few. If

---

75 *What do you do if your emotional intelligence is lacking when it comes to preparing for the future? (linkedin.com)*

you haven't done those exercises yet, or it's been a while and you'd like to revisit them, take time before reading further.

If you need more help evaluating your current emotional intelligence level, here are a few more activities you can try.

Emotional Scale [76]

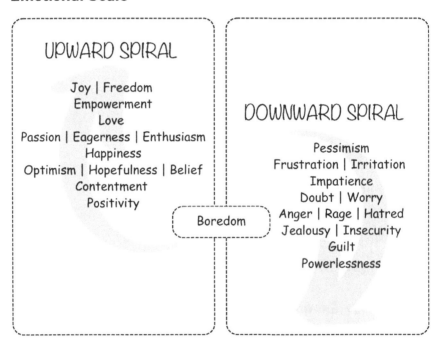

Evaluate your current emotional state on the scale. What actions can you take to move yourself to where you'd like to be to keep

---

76   *Assessing Emotional Intelligence: 19 Valuable Scales & PDFs (positivepsychology.com)*

the scale balanced? The Emotional Scale is handy in the mornings, when your emotions are fresh and not influenced by the day's activities. Use it each morning to establish a baseline of your emotional well-being.

Why not try the emotional intelligence activity to explore further?

 ## Emotional Intelligence Worksheet

Now that you've better understood your emotional intelligence, you are ready for step two: planning for your emotional future and setting realistic goals.

SET REALISTIC AND MEANINGFUL GOALS

What do you want to accomplish emotionally? Think short-term and long-term, and make a list. For right now, make the list as long as you want. Don't worry about how far-fetched or unrealistic a goal might seem; write everything down.

Once you've created your list, decide which are the most important. Pick two or three. Maybe your goals include developing better study habits, learning to say "No" more often when you don't want to do something, and being less annoyed at your sibling.

When choosing goals, use the acronym **SMART: specific, measurable, achievable, relevant, and time-bound.** Let's take developing better study habits as an example.

- **Specific:** Developing better study habits means creating a schedule, lessening distractions, and finding a spot in the house or outside the home (like the local library) where you regularly study.

- **Measurable:** You can measure this goal by tracking how many days you follow your schedule, noticing how often you are distracted and what those distractions are, and keeping track of how frequently you use your study spot and if it is useful. You can also measure if your study habits have improved by how much homework you are completing and the grades you are receiving.

- **Achievable**: Developing better study habits is an achievable goal.

- **Relevant:** Better study habits are a relatable goal because they will improve your school performance and help you develop time management and problem-solving skills, which you will need throughout your life.

- **Time-bound**: You have one week to develop your plan, and then you will follow it until your history final three weeks later and reassess your goal.

This example shows you how to use the acronym SMART to decide if your goal is right for you. You can apply SMART to any short- or long-term goal.

You won't achieve every goal you set because that would be impossible. When failure happens — and it will — you'll be prepared to handle that failure and disappointment because you've been regularly practicing your emotional intelligence skills.

Daily Practice of Emotional Intelligence Skills

Practice makes improvement.

In theory, the more you practice something, the better you become. Skills like ballet, piano, soccer, and cooking improve with practice. Everyone has a point at which they will peak with a skill, no matter how much work they put into it — and that's okay, because once you reach your peak, practice equals maintenance. Practice is how you keep the skills you worked hard to achieve at the level they should be.

Use a journal to record what's working and not working for you. Then, assess why specific techniques or skills aren't improving. For example, are you practicing meditation daily, but not feeling more relaxed? Maybe you need to lengthen the time you meditate, find a new spot, or sit or lie in a different, more comfortable way.

Use a mirror or record yourself when practicing skills that require speaking and body language. This way, you can watch yourself and make adjustments.

Breathing exercises, reframing negative thoughts, and grounding exercises can be done almost anywhere. Breathing in and out while counting from one to five in your head is helpful for calming nerves. You can reframe any negative thoughts, and an excellent grounding technique if you're feeling anxious or overwhelmed is to name one thing you can see, hear, feel, smell, taste, and touch.

For example: "I can see the trees outside the classroom." "I hear the clock ticking." "I feel the fleece of my sweatshirt." "I smell the cleaning solution used in the classroom." "I taste the gum I am chewing."

Learn and Grow from Your Mistakes

Learn to look at mistakes and failures as opportunities for growth and change. Failure is a part of life. It might feel disappointing, but you can still use it as an opportunity to learn and grow.

If your initial goal of being less annoyed at your sibling isn't working, think about what you could do differently. Could you talk to them about what bothers you? Think about the other options you can try, and then try again.

If your failures and disappointments are big, like not getting the lead you dreamed of in the school play or failing your driving test, take the time to grieve, reframe the situation, and try again. You can't go back in time and get the lead in this school play, but are there other places to audition? What about a local community theater? What other opportunities exist for performing? If there are none and you simply have to wait until the next school play, use the experience to practice emotional regulation.

Celebrate Your Successes and Progress

Your successes deserve celebration. If your goal was to use your new study habits to get an A on your history test, and you did just that, then celebrate! You can decide what a worthy reward is. You could give yourself the night off from homework, buy your favorite Starbucks drink, or go to the bookstore and pick out a new book.

Another way to celebrate your success is to tell people what you've achieved and be proud of your progress. If you've been working on calming your nerves or being more socially outgoing, share your results with others and talk about how you achieved your goals. Maybe you'll inspire someone else to focus on a new goal themselves!

Navigating Change

Change is inevitable. It happens to everyone. We experience small changes every day. You may have wanted vanilla creamer in your iced coffee, but someone used the last bit of it, so now you have to use plain. Perhaps you planned to wear your purple dress today but realized it's in the wash and had to choose something else. These are small changes we deal with every day.

But what about big changes? How do you handle major life changes, like moving to a new city, breaking up with your boyfriend, or switching schools?

These types of significant life changes can bring up some uncomfortable and confusing feelings.

The good news is that some of the very strategies you've already learned about for processing and handling emotions can also guide you through these major life changes.

Strategies for Managing Emotions During Significant Life Transitions

Strategies for managing your emotions during major life events are also known as coping skills. Life changes can bring about stress, anxiety, fear, and physical ailments.[77] Knowing what strategies are available and which work best before you need them can help you cope with a significant life change.

Journaling

Journaling is a fantastic hobby and skill for any emotional situation. It is private, expressive, and creative. You can write and say whatever is needed to help you process your feelings. Journaling also provides a reliable tool for looking back later if you need help understanding what you felt at the time.

Try a New Hobby

Refocus your energy by learning a new skill or hobby, or getting involved with an older hobby that's been dormant. Having another place to focus your thoughts and energy releases tension and can provide joy and contentment.

Taking up a new hobby is also the perfect way to meet new people. If your life change involves moving or switching schools, it can help you get to know people with common interests who may turn into friends!

77　*Life Transitions: 8 Effective Ways to Cope (copepsychology.com)*

Sleep

Getting enough good-quality sleep is vital for your emotional well-being.[78] Maintain a consistent sleep schedule and try to keep your sleep on track, even on the weekends. Most teenagers don't get enough sleep, which is another crucial reason to take sleep seriously.

Tweens and teens need at least 8–10 hours of sleep per night.[79] How much are you getting?

Lack of sleep impairs cognitive functioning, which affects memory, problem-solving skills, emotional regulation, and critical thinking.

Engage in Self-Care

Self-care is discussed a lot among parents, especially moms, but you need self-care, too! Life can be stressful for tweens and teens. Between school, friends, sports, music, church, and whatever else you have going on, there's a lot to stress you out.

Plus, in our world, most of us have 24/7 access to news and social media, which is not always good for our minds and self-care practice.

---

78   *8 Ways to Cope With Life Transitions | Psychology Today*

79   *Sleep for Teenagers | Sleep Foundation*

Self-care means engaging in anything that makes you feel happy and relaxed, and that relieves stress and anxiety[80]. That could include getting a haircut or your nails done, going for a bike ride or a jog, or binge-watching your favorite movie with a tub of Ben & Jerry's ice cream.

The only wrong way to do self-care is not to do it at all. Just like engaging in a hobby, self-care redirects your thoughts elsewhere and gives you time and space away from the emotions you are working to process.

Therapy

Therapy is a valuable tool for anyone at any age. You don't have to have a diagnosed mental health condition to see a therapist. If you're struggling with a significant life change, ask the school counselor for help.

If your parents would be open to the suggestion, ask them if they can help you find a therapist to talk to. Many therapists offer telehealth visits now, so it's possible to get care from the privacy of your bedroom.

---

80   *8 Ways to Cope With Life Transitions | Psychology Today*

Mindfulness

Like journaling, mindfulness is a versatile skill that can help you in most significant emotional situations. Mindfulness might mean doing a breathing exercise, closing your eyes and listening to music, walking in nature, or meditating. Meditation helps you be aware of the moment and reduces stress and anxiety. [81]

Mindfulness can be practiced in different ways, so explore options and see what feels right for you.

Activity: My Emotional Growth Plan for Setting and Achieving Emotional Growth Objectives

An emotional growth plan, also known as a personal development plan or individual development plan, is a plan used to develop your personal growth, self-awareness, and self-improvement. [82]

To successfully grow emotionally, you have to be committed to making changes. It's not enough to simply say you want to grow and change — you have to mean it!

---

81   *8 Ways to Cope With Life Transitions | Psychology Today*

82   *How to Create a Personal Development Plan: 3 Examples (positivepsychology.com)*

Key Notes:

- Commit to change. Make the commitment to yourself to grow and change emotionally.

- Avoid judging yourself. Being non-judgemental is key to accepting change and working through your emotions.

- Be honest and open. Trust yourself and the process.

- Avoid blame. Try not to blame yourself or others for your emotions. Situations and people can affect and change your emotions and growth, but it is important to avoid blaming others for your feelings and any obstacles you encounter.

Five Steps to Creating an Emotional Growth Plan

- Choose the area of development. What are the basic skills that you want to work on? Is it anger management, stress, or anxiety?

- Develop objectives and goals. What specifically do you want to do? For example, "I want to reduce my anxiety in social situations" or "I want to improve my response to situations that anger me."

- Choose the techniques or behaviors you will use. They might include breathing exercises, journaling, and art. You might also choose to exercise, meditate, and sleep more.

- What specific actions will you take to make these changes happen? For example, you could set a timer each day to ensure you get out for a walk on time, or go to the paper store to purchase a new journal and pen.

- Pick a review or completion date. How soon do you want to achieve this goal? Make sure it is realistic. Most changes need three to four weeks to cement new patterns.

REMEMBER!

You control your future and develop your future self. Other people will influence and affect you, but only you can commit to taking control of your emotions and responses to the world around you. Journaling, new hobbies, self-care, and therapy are all ways you can manage your emotions and work on your emotional growth.

CONCLUSION

Emotional development and expression are some of the most critical life skills you will ever develop. Without emotional skills, you cannot interact with the world and people around you in a healthy and successful way. Emotional skills support every aspect of your life. They foster social skills, cognitive development, and academic ability, and boost self-esteem and independence.

But even as you develop your emotional skills, remember there is always room for more growth. Emotional development is an ongoing skill that you can foster your whole life. *"A Tween Girl's Guide to Feelings & Emotions"* is a source you can return to again and again because emotional growth never stops.

The more you explore your emotions, the more you grow. When you face a new or uncomfortable emotional situation, you can turn to this guide for tips and tools.

As you grow and develop, your emotions and emotional capability will, too. If you find a tool no longer works the same way, return to the guide and try something new. Or, if you're experiencing an emotion you've never felt before or don't understand, revisit the emotions wheel to name it.

There are many ways to explore and process your emotions. The best part is that many of the tools you learned in this book apply to multiple situations! For example, if you love journaling, you can use it to understand, process, and express an emotion.

Your emotions are ever-changing, and are some of the incredibly unique things that make you who you are. No one else feels or experiences the world as you do, and that fact alone should remind you how important and valid your emotions are. No emotion you feel is ever wrong, even if it feels uncomfortable.

Every emotion you've ever felt or will feel is valid, unique, and entirely yours. No one else will feel exactly what you are feeling, which is why learning to understand your emotions is so vital. Your goal in life should be to learn, change, and continually grow from each new emotional experience.

Each skill you learn from this book will serve you elsewhere in your life. As you build upon your emotional intelligence, you will learn to love yourself, accept your failures, and celebrate your successes, becoming more independent and continually increasing your emotional well-being. Emotional growth is a never-ending journey that can accompany you no matter where your life takes you.

"Emotions are what make us human. Make us real. The word 'emotion' stands for energy in motion. Be truthful about your emotions, and use your mind and emotions in your favor, not against yourself."
— Robert T. Kiyosaki [83]

Good luck on the wonderful journey ahead.

83   Robert T. Kiyosaki Quote: "Emotions are what make us human. Make us real. The word 'emotion' stands for energy in motion. Be truthful about your em..." (quotefancy.com)

THANKS
FOR READING MY
BOOK!

I appreciate you picking this guide to empower your tweens with the skills they need to understand and manage their emotions confidently.

I would be so grateful if you could take a moment to leave an honest review or a star rating on Amazon.
(A star rating is just a couple of clicks away.)

By leaving a review, you'll help other parents discover this valuable resource for their own children. Thank you!

To leave a review & help spread the word

SCAN
HERE

Made in United States
Orlando, FL
15 March 2025

59478789R00098